# Socc[illegible] Pra[illegible]tice Games





[illegible]on

[illegible]D
[illegible]ach,
[illegible]h

**Library of Congress Cataloging-in-Publication Data**

Luxbacher, Joe.
Soccer practice games / Joe Luxbacher.-- 2nd ed.
p. cm.
ISBN 0-7360-4789-1 (soft cover)
1. Soccer--Training. 2. Soccer--Coaching. I. Title.
GV943.9.T7 L895 2003
796.334'07--dc21

2002153293

ISBN: 0-7360-4789-1



**Developmental Editor:** Laura Pulliam; **Assistant Editor:** Alisha Jeddeloh; **Copyeditor:** John Wentworth; **Proofreader:** Jennifer Davis; **Permission Manager:** Toni Harte; **Graphic Designer:** Nancy Rasmus; **Graphic Artist:** Tara Welsch; **Cover Designer:** Keith Blomberg; **Art and Photo Manager:** Dan Wendt; **Photographer (cover and interior):** © Human Kinetics; **Illustrators:** Roberto Sabas and Tim Offenstein; **Printer:** United Graphics

Human Kinetics books are available at special discounts for bulk purchase. Special editions or book excerpts can also be created to specification. For details, contact the Special Sales Manager at Human Kinetics.

Printed in the United States of America 10 9 8 7 6 5 4 3 2 1

**Human Kinetics**
Web site: www.HumanKinetics.com

*United States:* Human Kinetics
P.O. Box 5076, Champaign, IL 61825-5076
800-747-4457
e-mail: humank@hkusa.com

*Canada:* Human Kinetics
475 Devonshire Road Unit 100, Windsor, ON N8Y 2L5
800-465-7301 (in Canada only)
e-mail: orders@hkcanada.com

*Europe:* Human Kinetics
107 Bradford Road, Stanningley, Leeds LS28 6AT, United Kingdom
+44 (0) 113 255 5665
e-mail: hk@hkeurope.com

*Australia:* Human Kinetics
57A Price Avenue, Lower Mitcham, South Australia 5062
08 8277 1555
e-mail: liahka@senet.com.au

*New Zealand:* Human Kinetics
P.O. Box 105-231, Auckland Central
09-523-3462
e-mail: hkp@ihug.co.nz

To my late parents, Francis Luxbacher and Mary Ann Luxbacher,
the finest coaches a boy could ever ask for.
Their presence will always be with me.

And to my son, Travis, in hopes that he will derive as much
enjoyment from the game as I have.

# Contents

# Preface

Soccer! The game evokes an outpouring of passion and emotion unparalleled within the realm of competitive sport. Soccer provides a common language among people of diverse backgrounds and heritages, a bridge that spans economic, political, cultural, and religious barriers. Known as football throughout most of the world, soccer is the national sport of nearly every country in Asia, Africa, Europe, and South America. It remains the only football-type game played at the Olympics. Millions more people follow the World Cup, soccer's international championship, than follow North America's baseball World Series.

Consider the following statistics. Soccer is played daily by an estimated 1.2 billion people—nearly one-fifth of the world's population! More than 150 million registered athletes, including 10 million women, play the sport on an annual basis. Millions more kick the ball around on an unofficial basis—on the sandlots, in school yards, and on the back streets of small towns and large cities. Over the course of each year, one million referees officiate an estimated 20 million matches. Billions (yes, billions) of fans fervently follow their favorite teams and players by attending games or viewing the action on television and through other media outlets. Upward of 35 million cumulative television viewers tuned in at one time or another to watch the 2002 World Cup games played in South Korea and Japan. Nearly 2 billion people watched live as Brazil downed Germany 2-0 in the final, a number that dwarfs the television audience of the NFL Super Bowl. These numbers point directly to the fact that soccer is, without question, the world's most popular game.

Soccer's universal appeal lies in the nature of the game itself. With the exception of the goalkeeper, there are no specialists on the soccer field. As in basketball and hockey, each player must be able to defend as well as attack. Although players don't have to be a particular size or shape, all must possess a high level of fitness because the action is virtually nonstop, with no time outs. Field players are required to run several miles during the course of a match, with much of that distance at sprint pace. Players must perform a variety of foot skills under the match pressures of restricted space, limited time, physical fatigue, and the determined challenge of opponents.

Decision-making abilities are constantly tested as players must respond to rapidly changing situations during play. A thorough understanding of tactics and strategies is essential. The physical and mental challenges confronting players are many and great. Individual and ultimately team performance depends on each player's ability to meet these challenges. Such ability does not occur by chance—it must be developed. Only through players and coaches working in concert can we achieve that objective.

An old adage among coaches says that "the game is the best teacher." *Soccer Practice Games* was written with that in mind. The book provides a wide range of training games to nurture the technical, tactical, and physical development of players. All the exercises are designed to challenge players and keep them active, motivated, and thoroughly involved. The games are competitive and fun to play, and they can be easily adapted to many ages and abilities. While standard drills are an important part of a team's training regimen, it's no secret that novice and experienced players alike respond most favorably if they're excited and enthused about what they're doing. The games included here are designed to create such an attitude. One of coaching's richest rewards is to watch your players enjoy themselves as they blossom under your guidance. The games in this book will help make that happen.

# Acknowledgments

The teamwork required to produce a quality soccer team can be likened to the collective effort that goes into the writing and publishing of a book. In that regard, I'm deeply indebted to many individuals for their help with this project. Although it's not possible to mention everyone by name, I would like to express my sincere appreciation to the staff at Human Kinetics, particularly Ted Miller and Laura Pulliam, for their patience and support in the development of the book; to Bunya Retzloff, friend, colleague, and student of the game, for providing several new and innovative games to the skill and tactical sections of the book; to the staff of Shoot to Score Soccer Academy, for their willingness to share thoughts and ideas; and last but certainly not least, to my lovely wife, Gail, for her constant love and support of everything that I do.

Thanks so much to all of you.

# Make Practice Games Work For You

Planning a practice that motivates players to learn, train hard, and most important, enjoy the game is a fundamental responsibility of the soccer coach. Players of all ages and ability levels want to be excited, enthused, and entertained while they learn. They won't respond well to long-winded lectures, standing in line, or anything that spells boredom. They want to become better players, but they also want to have a good time in the process. Young soccer players in particular derive the most benefit from practices that are challenging and fun, from exercises that are activity oriented, and from games in which they are constantly moving, touching the ball, and scoring goals. *Soccer Practice Games* was written with this in mind.

The book contains 125 game-simulated activities that coaches can use to create an optimal practice environment. The games teach fundamentals and focus on the skills and tactics required to become a more complete soccer player. Players are placed in controlled competitive situations that provide everyone an opportunity to succeed. The games are particularly useful for beginning and intermediate players and can be adapted to accommodate more traditional training with experienced players.

The book is organized into six parts: Warm-Up and Conditioning Games; Passing and Receiving Games; Dribbling, Shielding, and Tackling Games; Heading and Shooting Games; Tactical Training Games; and Goalkeeper Training Games. Although categorized by their primary focus, most games emphasize two or more essential elements of the sport. For example, all games contained in Part V (Tactical Training) require players to move continuously while dribbling, passing, or receiving the ball. As a result, players benefit from fitness and skill development, in addition to the tactical concepts contained in these games. When possible, the games in Part II through Part V have been loosely grouped in order of increasing complexity. This sequence is provided to assist coaches in selecting games most appropriate for their players. Expose beginning players to the basic games first. As your players become more confident and competent, gradually progress to more mentally and physically challenging games. Experienced players derive greater benefit from games that simulate the conditions faced in match situations—pressures such as limited space and time and being challenged by opponents. Keep in mind that most games included here are versatile and can be adapted to the age and ability of players. For example, coaches can make a game more challenging by

- imposing restrictions, such as requiring one- or two-touch passing only,
- manipulating the space and time in which players have to execute skills or make decisions (the less space and time available the more difficult the challenge),
- increasing physical demands by requiring more running and player movement,
- incorporating decision-making into the exercise, such as requiring players to choose from one of several options when passing or receiving the ball, and
- including the ultimate challenge: the pressure of determined opponents.

Best of all, whether a game is intended to test the novice or challenge the experienced player, the activity remains fun and functional for everyone involved. Each game is organized in an easily understood format, as described below.

**Title.** In most cases, but not all, the title provides a general idea of what the game involves and emphasizes. For example, Dribble the Maze and Score requires players to dribble through an obstacle course before shooting on goal. Some titles are not as obvious, however, and the coach should look to other sections, such as Objectives, for more information on what the game involves.

**Minutes.** A time frame is listed for each game. This is provided as a general guideline only and should be adjusted to the age, ability, and physical maturity of your players. The duration of a game is ultimately your decision, since you know your players better than anyone else.

**Players.** Some games require a specific number of players, while others do not. For example, Play the Wall requires three players because the entire focus is on the 2 vs 1 situation. Other games, such as Chain Gang or Connect the Dots, might involve a range in the number of players. When determining how many players to include in a game, keep in mind that all players should be active throughout the activity and touching the ball most of the time. If too many players or too few balls are involved, the game won't accomplish your objectives.

**Objectives.** Most games have a primary objective and two or more closely associated secondary objectives. For example, the primary objective of the game All Versus All is the development of dribbling skills. Secondary objectives include the development of shielding and tackling skills, as well as improving fitness. Choosing games that accomplish more than one objective makes the best use of limited practice time.

Coaches should also consider a game's objectives to determine whether the game fits into the general theme of a specific practice session. For example, if the primary focus of training is to develop passing and receiving skills, the games selected for the session should fit that criterion.

**Setup.** Field dimensions, equipment, and any other special needs are listed under this heading. Balls, cones, flags, and colored vests are some of the most common equipment items the games call for. Field dimensions are provided only as general guidelines and should be adjusted to the number and ability of your players.

**Procedure.** This section gives a brief overview of how the game is played. In some instances, you or an assistant coach might act as server or scorekeeper while observing the action, but that is not always necessary. The majority of games are designed so that players can use their own initiative and decision-making abilities to organize the action and get play started.

**Scoring.** When appropriate, a scoring system has been provided to add an element of competition to the game. It should be clearly understood, however, that the ultimate aim of each game is for players to challenge themselves to achieve a higher standard of performance. Improvement is the true barometer of success, not who wins or loses a practice game.

**Practice tips.** These suggestions are provided to help you organize the games in the most efficient and effective manner. Most tips concern possible adjustments in the size of the playing area or restrictions placed on the players. Safety and liability concerns are also addressed in this section.

# Planning Practice Sessions

The following guidelines apply to players of all ages and ability levels and are provided here to help coaches plan their practice sessions. Keep in mind that these are suggestions only and should be adapted to accommodate the needs of your individual players.

**Create a positive training atmosphere.** Whether you're working with elementary-school kids or seasoned professionals, a boring practice is a poor learning environment. For the most part, training should be fun. Through careful planning and creative thinking, coaches at all levels can provide stimulating, highly motivated training sessions to achieve their specific learning objectives.

**Consider the players under your charge.** Plan a realistic practice—one that challenges players but is also within their physical and mental capabilities. Consider your players' ages, abilities, and developmental levels. Beginning players may have difficulty executing even the most fundamental skills, so it's important that you don't place them in situations where they have little or no chance of achieving success.

**Develop a theme.** It's a mistake, particularly with younger players, to try to cover many topics in a single practice session. Center each practice on an underlying theme. For example, the primary objective of a training session might be improved passing and receiving skills or to create goal-scoring opportunities through creative dribbling. Organize your practice around a variety of exercises and games related to this central theme.

**Keep your players moving.** The more times a player can pass, receive, shoot, head, or dribble the ball, the more likely he or she will enjoy the practice and improve skills. Make sure that a large supply of balls, ideally one for each player, is available. An ample supply of balls provides many more options regarding choice of drills and practice games and makes training more enjoyable since players are constantly moving and touching the ball. The easiest way to guarantee a sufficient number of balls is to require each player to bring a ball to practice. Just as baseball players bring their glove to the field, soccer players should bring a ball.

**Simplicity is bliss.** Much of soccer's inherent beauty rests in the fact that it's a very simple game. Keep it that way! Complicated drills or highly intricate training exercises only confuse and frustrate your players. When planning practices, always take into consideration the "KISS" principle of coaching—*Keep It Simple, Stupid!*

**Build a foundation.** Each drill or exercise should lay the groundwork for those that follow. Begin the session with basic activities, and progress to more match-like situations. For example, you might begin practice with simple passing drills involving minimal player movement and gradually progress to exercises where your players must pass and receive the ball while moving at game speed under the pressure of challenging opponents. Where to start in the progression depends on the ability and experience of your players. Higher-level players will naturally begin with more demanding exercises than novice players. In both cases, however, organize your drills so that each serves as a natural lead-in for the next.

**Don't overcoach.** Practice sessions as well as the games themselves should center on the players, not the coaches. Use brief demonstrations and simple explanations, and then get your players actively involved. Avoid long lines, long stops in play, and long speeches. Stop the action to provide specific and appropriate feedback but only at opportune times.

**Ensure a safe training environment.** Soccer is a contact sport and involves some physical risk. Accidental collisions, bumps, and bruises sometimes occur. To minimize injuries, make every effort to give your players a safe practice environment. This includes adequate supervision and planning, matching players with others of similar size and ability, and establishing guidelines for appropriate behavior.

It's imperative that players wear appropriate equipment during practice and games. To prevent lower leg injuries, both field players and goalkeepers should wear shin guards. Most guards are made of light, flexible plastic and are inexpensive. Goalkeepers should wear position-specific equipment as well. Padded shorts or full-length pants are recommended, particularly when training and playing on hard natural surfaces or artificial turf. Both shorts and pants should have padding over the hip area.

Use common sense when selecting soccer goals. Despite their heavy weight, portable full-size goals (8 feet high by 24 feet wide) can topple over if not properly anchored, particularly if youngsters hang on the crossbar. Solid, professionally-made goals firmly secured to the ground are recommended, but they are also expensive. If cost is an issue, and for most of us it is, use cones, flags, or other kinds of markers to represent goals.

**Practice economical training methods.** To make the most effective use of your limited practice time, incorporate elements of fitness, skill, or tactics into each exercise. Toward that aim, include a ball in every drill or exercise, even those designed primarily to improve fitness. However long the practice, make sure that it's time well spent. Quality is much more important than quantity when it comes to duration of a training session.

**End with a game.** When all's said and done, the game itself is still the best teacher. End each practice with a match or a simulated match situation. The match need not be full-sided (11 v 11). Small-sided games (3 v 3 up to 6 v 6) are more beneficial in some ways. Playing with fewer numbers per team allows players more opportunities to touch the ball. They are required to make more decisions, which aids their tactical development. The emphasis on positional play is greatly reduced because each player must defend as well as attack, which promotes total player development. Last but not least, the number of scoring chances is greatly increased in small-sided games, which makes them more fun for everyone involved.

# Part I

# Warm-Up and Conditioning Games

Warm-up activities serve several important functions. They raise muscle temperature and increase suppleness, promote increased blood flow and oxygen supply, improve muscular contraction and reflex time, and help prevent muscle strains and next-day soreness. The duration and intensity of the warm-up can vary from one practice to the next, and from one team to another, depending on individual needs. Generally, players should warm up enough to begin sweating, which indicates that muscle temperatures have elevated. This might take anywhere from 10 to 30 minutes, depending on the temperature, humidity, and general environmental conditions. Obviously, players won't have to warm up as hard or as long on a hot, humid day in August as they will on a cold, blustery day in December.

Any form of activity that involves repeated action of large muscle groups can be used in the warm-up. Traditional exercises include stretches coupled with old favorites such as jumping jacks, sit-ups, push-ups, and knee-bends. This type of warm-up is commonly called an "unrelated" warm-up because it does not involve soccer-specific movements. While nothing is inherently wrong with an unrelated warm-up, players typically prefer a soccer-specific warm-up, which is more appropriate from both a mental and physical perspective. A soccer-specific warm-up might include skill-related warm-up games that involve passing or dribbling skills or might take the form of games that stress movement, mobility, and agility. The games described in this part are intended to add variety and spice to the warm-up while achieving the primary objective of preparing players for the vigorous training to follow. Since most of the games (though not all) have players use one or more soccer balls, skill development is an added benefit of these games.

Physical conditioning can be maintained, and in some cases improved, through many of the games described in this section. Essential components of soccer-specific fitness include flexibility and agility, mobility and balance, aerobic and anaerobic endurance, muscular strength, speed, and power. Players can improve soccer-specific speed by performing exercises that require sudden changes of speed and direction along with deceptive body movements. Quickness, balance, and an ability to change direction suddenly are as important to a soccer player as straight-out sprinting speed.

# 1 Two-Touch Pass and Follow

**Minutes:** 10

**Players:** 5

**Objective:** To incorporate two-touch passing into a warm-up activity

**Setup:** Use markers to outline a 20-yard square. Station one player at the midpoint of each sideline. Station the fifth player in the center of the square with the ball.

**Procedure:** To begin, the central player passes the ball to one of the sideline players and sprints to that spot. The sideline player receives and prepares the ball with the first touch, passes to another player with the second touch, and sprints to that spot. Players continue passing and following the pass at maximum speed.

**Scoring:** None

**Practice tips:** Emphasize a quality first touch; the ball should be controlled and prepared in one movement. Encourage players to make hard sprints in support of their pass, just as they would in a game situation.

# 2 Circle Dribble

**Minutes:** 10

**Players:** 6 to 12 (2 teams of equal number)

**Objectives:** To develop dribbling skills; to improve fitness

**Setup:** Play within the center circle of a regulation field. Form two teams of equal number. Pair each player with an opponent from the opposing team, and assign each pair a number (1, 2, and so on). Players position on the perimeter of the circle directly across from their opponent. One player of each pair has a ball.

**Procedure:** Begin by calling out a pair number, such as "1." The two number 1 players then immediately sprint counterclockwise around the perimeter of the circle, the one with the ball dribbling and the other pursuing. The player with the ball attempts to dribble around the circle and back to his or her space before being tagged by the chaser. As soon as both players return to their original positions, call a different pair number. Partners exchange possession of the ball after each circuit. Continue calling pairs at random.

**Scoring:** Award a point to the player who dribbles around the circle and back to his or her space before being tagged. The team scoring the most points wins.

**Practice tips:** Adjust the playing area to match the age and ability of your players. The circumference of the circle should be such that the chaser has a reasonable chance of catching the dribbler. As a variation, call out two numbers to participate simultaneously.

# 3 Speed Dribble Relay

**Minutes:** 10 to 15

**Players:** Unlimited (equal-sized teams of 4 to 6)

**Objectives:** To develop dribbling speed; to improve fitness

**Setup:** Use the sideline or endline of the field as a starting line. Position teams side by side behind the starting line, with at least three yards between teams. Place a flag or marker 25 yards in front of each team. Give the first player in line for each team a ball.

**Procedure:** On the coach's command, the first player dribbles quickly around the flag and back to the starting line, where he or she exchanges the ball with the next player in line. All team members dribble around the flag in turn. The team completing the relay in the shortest time wins. Repeat 10 times with a short rest between each race.

**Scoring:** The winning team gets 3 points, second place 2 points, and third place 1 point. The team totaling the most points after 10 races wins the event.

**Practice tips:** The technique a player uses to dribble in open space should differ from that used when dribbling for close control in a crowd of players. Players should push the ball several steps ahead with the outside surface of the foot, sprint to catch up to it, and push it again. Adjust the total distance covered to accommodate the age and fitness level of players.

# 4 Pinball Wizards

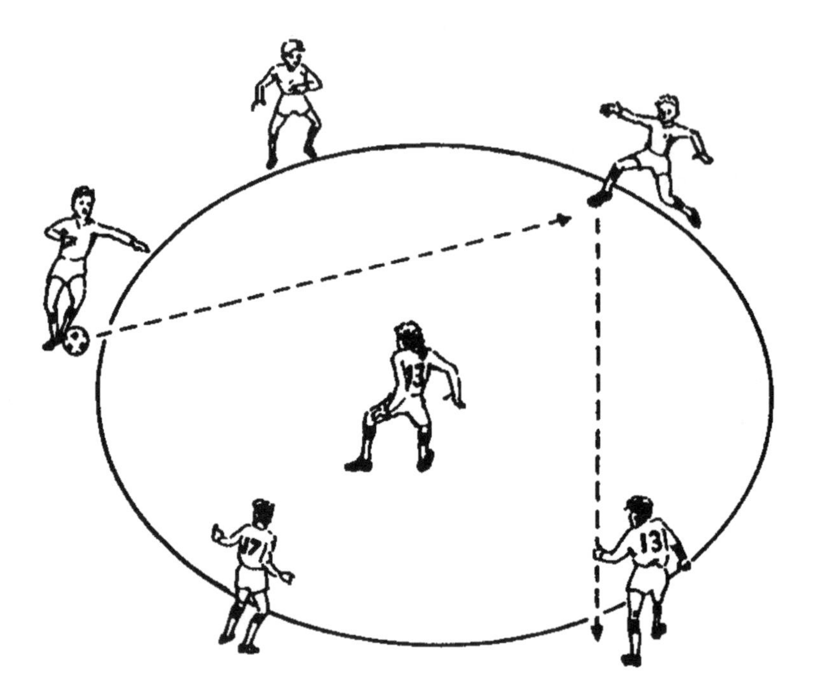

**Minutes:** 10 to 15

**Players:** 6 (5 attackers; 1 defender)

**Objectives:** To develop one-touch passing technique; to warm up players before moving to more vigorous training

**Setup:** Use markers to form a circle about 12 yards in diameter. Station a defender within the circle; position five attackers evenly spaced along the circle perimeter. Give one of the attackers a ball.

**Procedure:** Attackers keep the ball from the defender by passing among themselves. Attackers are allowed to move laterally along the perimeter of the circle but may not move inward within the circle. Attackers must execute one-touch passes only (thus the name, "pinball wizards"). If the ball goes out of the circle because of an errant pass, or if the defender intercepts a pass, the ball is immediately returned to an attacker, and the game continues.

**Scoring:** Award 1 point for eight consecutive passes without a loss of possession. Award the defender 1 point for stealing the ball and for each time the ball goes out of the circle. Play to 10, then switch defenders. Repeat the game until each player has defended.

**Practice tips:** To make the game more challenging for advanced players, station two defenders in the circle. For less skilled players, enlarge the circle or permit two-touch passing.

# 5 Across-the-Circle Sprint

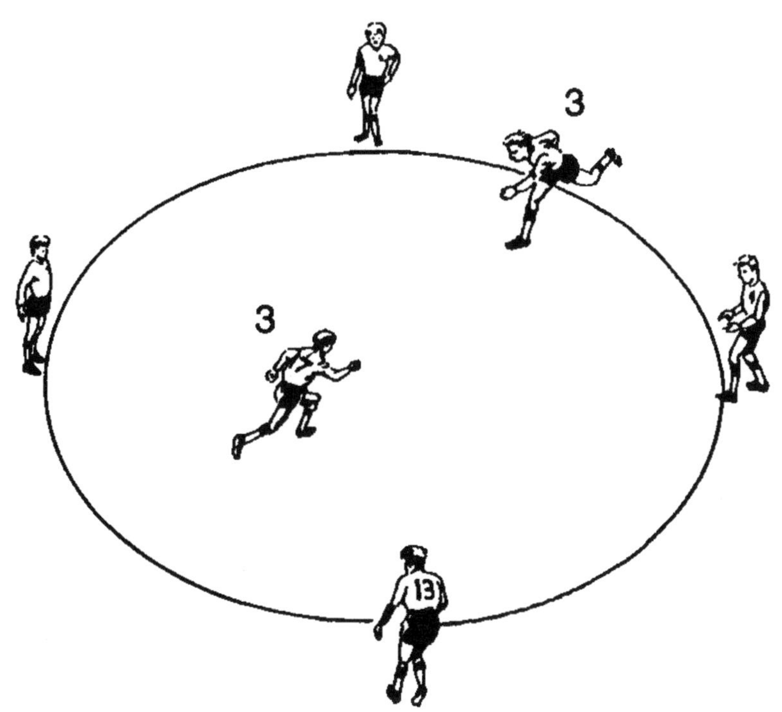


**Minutes:** 10

**Players:** 6 to 12 (2 teams of equal number)

**Objectives:** To improve running form; to develop endurance

**Setup:** Use the center circle of the field as the playing area. Pair each player with an opponent, and number each pair (1, 2, and so on). Players position on the perimeter of the circle directly opposite their partners.

**Procedure:** Begin by calling out a pair number, such as "3." The two number 3 players then switch positions by sprinting across the circle. The goal is to reach their opponent's space on the circle before he or she arrives at their spot. Continue to call out pair numbers at random. You might want to call out two numbers in quick succession so that four players are running at once.

**Scoring:** None

**Practice tips:** Adjust the size of the circle to match the fitness level of the players. You can increase the physical demands of the exercise by having players run across the circle and then back to their original spot.

# 6 Flag Tag

**Minutes:** 10

**Players:** Unlimited

**Objective:** To incorporate dribbling skills into your warm-up

**Setup:** Play within the penalty area. Each player tucks a colored flag into the back of his or her shorts. At least half the flag should be hanging out.

**Procedure:** Players begin dribbling among themselves within the penalty area. On your command, the game begins. Players dribble after other players and try to steal their flags while also keeping their own flag safe from other players. All players should keep their own flag tucked into the back of their shorts, while holding stolen flags in their hand as they dribble about. Players dribble the ball under close control at all times; they may not leave their ball to chase after an opponent. Play several games.

**Scoring:** The player who ends up with the most stolen flags while retaining his or her own flag wins the game.

**Practice tips:** As a variation, have players perform a dribbling move (such as a step-over or a chop) after they steal an opponent's flag.

# 7 Hounds and Hares

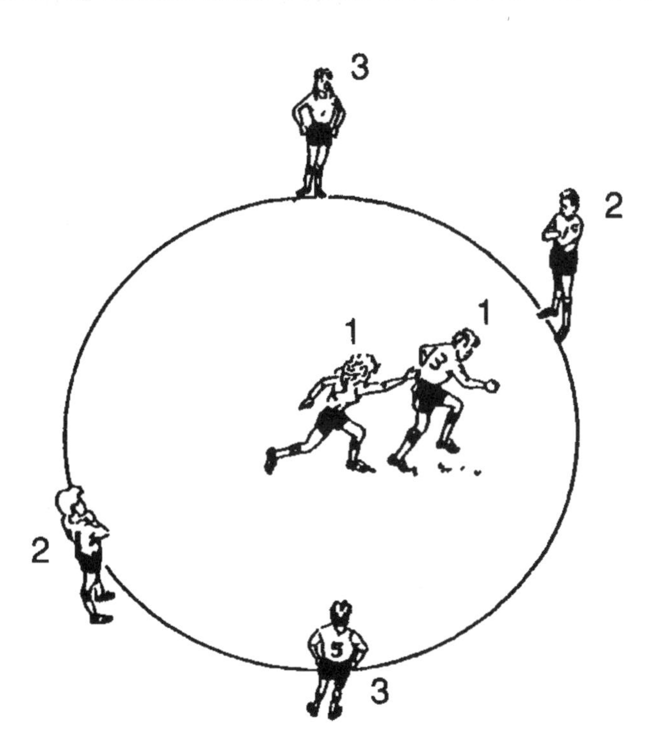


**Minutes:** 10 (multiple 60- to 90-second rounds)

**Players:** 6 to 8 (in pairs)

**Objective:** To develop mobility, agility, and deceptive body feints while improving fitness

**Setup:** Play within the center circle of a regulation field. Arrange players into pairs and assign each pair a number (1, 2, and so on). Partners position on the perimeter of the circle directly opposite each other. Designate one partner as the "hound" and the other as the "hare." No balls are required.

**Procedure:** Begin the game by calling out a number, such as "1." The number 1 players then enter the circle. The hound immediately gives chase and attempts to tag the hare. If the hare is tagged, players reverse roles immediately. Play continuously for 60 to 90 seconds, and then call a different pair into the circle. The initial hound and hare return to their original positions on the perimeter and rest.

**Scoring:** None

**Practice tips:** This is a physically demanding game when played at full intensity. The hare should use quick changes of speed and direction to elude the hound. Make the game more challenging by lengthening the duration of each round or increasing the size of the circle. As a variation, call two or three pairs into the circle at the same time.

# 8 Chain Gang

**Minutes:** 10

**Players:** Unlimited

**Objectives:** To improve mobility and agility; to develop endurance

**Setup:** Use markers to outline a rectangular area 30 yards by 40 yards. Designate two players as "it," who position outside the area. All remaining "free" players station within the rectangle.

**Procedure:** The players who are "it" enter the area to chase after and tag free players. Free players are allowed to move anywhere within the field area to avoid being tagged. A free player who is tagged must join hands with the player who tagged him or her to form a chain. As more players are tagged, the chains grow longer. Only two chains are permitted at any one time (the original chains may not split into smaller chains). Chains can work together to corner or trap free players. Continue until only two free players remain. Repeat the game with those two players being "it" to begin the next round.

**Scoring:** The last two remaining free players win the game.

**Practice tips:** Vary the size of the area or the number of chains allowed depending on the number of players. Free players should use sudden changes of speed and direction coupled with deceptive body feints to avoid being tagged.

# 9 Hunt the Fox

**Minutes:** 10 to 15

**Players:** 10 to 20 (2 equal-sized teams of 5 to 10)

**Objectives:** To improve endurance; to coordinate the support movement used to create successful passing combinations

**Setup:** Use markers to outline an area 40 yards by 50 yards. Divide the group into two teams of equal number. Station both teams within the area. Use colored scrimmage vests to differentiate teams. Designate one player on each team as a "fox," who wears distinctive clothing (hat, shirt, or vest). Each team has possession of a ball to begin.

**Procedure:** Players pass the ball by throwing (and catching)—not kicking it. The object is to hit the opposing fox below the knees with a thrown ball. The fox is free to move anywhere within the area to avoid being hit. A player is permitted five or fewer steps with the ball before releasing it to a teammate or throwing at the fox. Teammates can protect their fox by blocking or deflecting opponent's throws. Change of possession occurs when a pass is intercepted by a member of the opposing team, the ball drops to the ground, or a player takes too many steps with the ball. Players may not wrestle the ball from an opponent. Have two balls in play at all times.

**Scoring:** A team scores 1 point each time a player hits the opposing fox with a thrown ball below the knees. The team scoring the most points wins.

**Practice tips:** Encourage short, accurate passes (tosses) with a high likelihood of completion. Attacking players should continually adjust their position to provide multiple passing options for the teammate with the ball. Repeat the game several times, with different players being the foxes.

# 10 Piggyback Soccer

**Minutes:** 15

**Players:** 8 to 20 (2 teams of equal number)

**Objectives:** To develop muscular strength and endurance; to spice up the training session

**Setup:** Use markers to outline an area 25 yards by 40 yards. Position a small goal (three to five yards wide) at the midpoint of each endline. Pair each player with a teammate of comparable size and weight. Use colored scrimmage vests to differentiate teams. One team has the ball to begin.

**Procedure:** Begin with a kickoff from the center of the field. Each team defends a goal and can score in the opponent's goal. Each player must carry his or her partner piggyback fashion during play. Partners change positions every 30 to 60 seconds to share the burden of carrying each other. There are no goalkeepers. Otherwise, regular soccer rules apply.

**Scoring:** Points are scored by kicking the ball through the opponent's goal. The team scoring the most points wins.

**Practice tips:** This game is appropriate only for physically mature players of high school age and older and is not suitable for young players who lack sufficient strength and coordination. It's important to match players with a partner of similar size and weight to avoid mismatches.

# 11 Dribble the Gauntlet

**Minutes:** 10 to 15

**Players:** Unlimited

**Objective:** To incorporate passing and dribbling skills in a warm-up activity

**Setup:** Use markers to outline an area 25 by 40 yards, with a safety zone 5 yards deep at each end. Station three "marksmen" in the center of the field, each with a ball. All remaining players, each with a ball, station in a safety zone facing the marksmen.

**Procedure:** On your command, the players in the safety zone attempt to dribble the length of the field into the opposite safety zone. Marksmen "capture" the dribblers by contacting them below the knees with a passed ball. All passes must be made with the inside or outside surface of the foot; no shooting is permitted. A dribbler who is contacted below the waist with a passed ball, or who loses control of his or her ball outside the field boundaries, is considered captured and joins the marksmen for the next round. Dribblers who reach the safety zone remain there until the coach issues the command to return to the original safety zone. Players dribble back and forth between safety zones until all but three have been captured. These players are marksmen for the next game.

**Scoring:** The last three players to avoid capture are the winners.

**Practice tips:** Adjust the area to match the ages, abilities, and number of your players. Encourage marksmen to dribble close to their targets before passing the ball.

# 12 Team Nutmeg

**Minutes:** 10 (4 periods, $2\frac{1}{2}$ minutes each)

**Players:** Unlimited (2 teams of equal number)

**Objectives:** To warm the muscles and prepare the body for more vigorous training; to improve your players' ability to dribble for close control in a confined area

**Setup:** Use markers to outline an area 25 by 30 yards. Team 1 players position as stationary targets with their feet spread two to three feet apart at various spots within the playing area. Team 2 players, each with a ball, position outside the area.

**Procedure:** Team 2 players dribble into the area and attempt to push pass their ball through the legs of as many team 1 players as possible during a $2\frac{1}{2}$-minute round. This dribbling maneuver is called a "nutmeg" and, in real games, is the ultimate embarrassment for a defender. Team 1 players must remain stationary during the $2\frac{1}{2}$-minute round. A player may not nutmeg the same opponent twice in succession. Teams reverse roles for the second round and for each successive round. Play at least four rounds.

**Scoring:** Players compete against teammates, using the honor system to tally scores. Each player counts the number of nutmegs he or she performs in the allotted time. The player with the most nutmegs wins the round.

**Practice tips:** Adjust the playing area size to accommodate the number of players. Stationary players should not position too close together to avoid collisions among dribblers.

# 13 Leapfrog Races

**Minutes:** 10

**Players:** Unlimited (equal-sized teams of 4 to 6)

**Objectives:** To develop upper body strength and endurance; to develop leg strength and power; to create an enjoyable practice atmosphere

**Setup:** Designate a start line and a finish line 50 yards apart. Organize teams of equal number. Teammates position in single file behind the starting line, with at least five yards between teams. The first player (1) in each line bends forward at the waist and crouches with knees flexed and hands placed slightly above the knees. This is the "frog" position.

**Procedure:** At your call of "Go!" player 2 places his or her hands on player 1's upper back and leapfrogs over him or her. Player 2 immediately assumes the frog position a couple of feet ahead of player 1. Player 3 then leapfrogs over players 1 and 2 and assumes a frog position in front of player 2, and so on. Teammates continue leapfrogging over one another until they reach the finish line. Complete five races, with a short rest between each.

**Scoring:** The first team to get all players across the finish line wins.

**Practice tips:** Leapfrog races are most appropriate for physically mature players with enough upper body and leg strength. Increase or decrease the physical demands of the game by lengthening or shortening the race distance. In addition to developing muscular strength and endurance, leapfrog races can create much laughter and helps form camaraderie among players.

# 14 Attack of the Crab Monsters

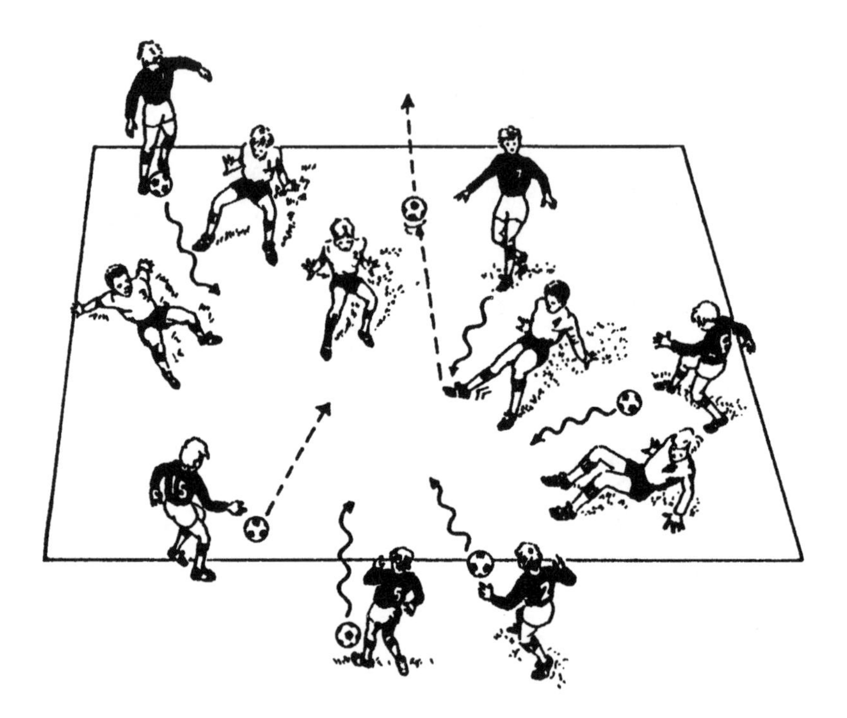

**Minutes:** 3 per round (repeated several times)

**Players:** 11 to 20

**Objective:** To develop dribbling skills within an enjoyable training atmosphere

**Setup:** Use markers to outline a rectangular area 20 yards by 30 yards. Designate five players to be "crabs," who station within the area. Crabs must move about in a crabwalk (a sitting position with weight supported by hands and feet). Remaining players station outside the area, each with a ball.

**Procedure:** Players outside the area enter to dribble among the crabs. The crabs crawl after the dribblers and attempt to kick their balls out of the area. Crabs must move about in the crab position and may not use their hands to play the ball. Dribblers use quick changes of speed and direction, coupled with deceptive body feints, to elude the crabs. Crabs can work together to reduce the space and force dribblers into errors. A player whose ball is kicked out of the area is eliminated from the game; he or she practices juggling until the game concludes. Continue until all dribblers have been eliminated, then repeat the game with different players as crabs.

**Scoring:** Crabs get 1 point for each ball kicked out of the area. The crab with the most points wins.

**Practice tips:** To make the game more challenging, reduce the area size or increase the number of crabs. Caution dribblers not to step on the crabs' hands.

# 15 Dribble Freeze Tag

**Minutes:** 3 per round (several rounds)

**Players:** Unlimited

**Objective:** To rehearse dribbling skills in a warm-up activity within an enjoyable training atmosphere

**Setup:** Use markers to outline an area 25 yards by 30 yards. Designate two players as chasers, who position outside the area without balls. All remaining players ("free" players) station within the area, each with a ball.

**Procedure:** Free players dribble randomly within the area. The two chasers enter the area to chase after and tag the free players, who must dribble a ball at all times. A player who is tagged is considered "frozen" and must sit on his or her ball. Free players can release those who are frozen by dribbling close and touching them on the shoulder. The game continues for three minutes or until all players are frozen, whichever comes first. Repeat the game several times, with different chasers for each game.

**Scoring:** Chaser gets 1 point for each player tagged. The chaser who scores the most points wins the round.

**Practice tips:** This is an excellent dribbling exercise for beginning players. Adjust the size of the playing area to accommodate the ages and number of your players. Older players will need more space than younger players.

# 16 Team Tag

**Minutes:** 10-15

**Players:** 12 to 16 (4 equal-sized teams)

**Objective:** To develop dribbling skills in a warm-up activity

**Setup:** Use markers to outline an area 25 yards by 40 yards. Station all four teams within the area, each player with a ball. Designate one team as "it." Use colored scrimmage vests to differentiate teams.

**Procedure:** Players on the "it" team chase after and attempt to tag players from the other teams. All players, including the chasers, must dribble a ball as they move within the field area. Any player tagged is eliminated from the game and leaves the field to practice juggling. Players who are "it" can't leave their ball to tag opponents—they must keep the ball under close control at all times. The game ends when all opponents have been eliminated or after five minutes, whichever comes first. Play four games, using different chasers for each game.

**Scoring:** The team that eliminates all its opponents in the least amount of time wins.

**Practice tips:** Reduce the field area for younger players.

# 17 Crabs and Minnows

**Minutes:** 10-15

**Players:** Unlimited

**Objective:** To develop dribbling skills in a warm-up activity

**Setup:** Use markers to outline an area 20 yards by 30 yards, with a safety zone 3 yards wide at each end spanning the width of the field. Designate three players to be "crabs," who station, without balls, in the center of the area. Crabs assume the crab position (sitting with body off the ground supported by arms and legs). Remaining players ("minnows") station in one of the safety zones, each with a ball.

**Procedure:** On command, the minnows attempt to dribble ("swim") the length of the area into the opposite safety zone. Crabs try to prevent this by kicking the minnows' balls out of the playing area. Crabs must remain in the crab position and can't use their hands to play the ball. Minnows who dribble successfully from one safety zone into the other remain there until the coach gives the signal to return to the original safety zone. A minnow whose ball is kicked out of the area becomes a crab for the next round. Minnows continue dribbling from one safety zone to the other at your command, until only three minnows remain. These players are crabs to begin the next game.

**Scoring:** None

**Practice tips:** Minnows can't chip the ball over the crabs in an effort to reach the safety zone—they must dribble between or around the crabs. Reduce the field width to make the game more challenging for the minnows.

# 18 Join the Hunt

**Minutes:** 10 to 15

**Players:** 10 to 20

**Objectives:** To practice passing and dribbling skills in a warm-up exercise; to develop agility and mobility

**Setup:** Use markers to form a field about 30 yards by 40 yards. Designate three players as "hunters," who station outside the area, each with a ball. Remaining players ("free" players) station within the area, without balls. Have a supply of balls, one for each player, along the perimeter of the playing area.

**Procedure:** At your command, the hunters enter the area to dribble after and contact free players below the knees with a passed ball. Free players may move anywhere within the area to avoid being hit. Any free player hit by a ball below the knee immediately collects one of the loose balls from the perimeter of the area and joins the hunt. Continue until all free players have been eliminated. Repeat several times, with different hunters to begin each game.

**Scoring:** None

**Practice tips:** Adjust the area size to accommodate the ages, abilities, and number of players. Encourage hunters to dribble close to their targets before passing. This helps develop dribbling skills and also increases the likelihood of an accurate pass. As a variation, require hunters to use a specific type of pass (such as inside-of-foot or instep passes only) or have them use their weakest foot to pass the ball.

# 19 Team Handball

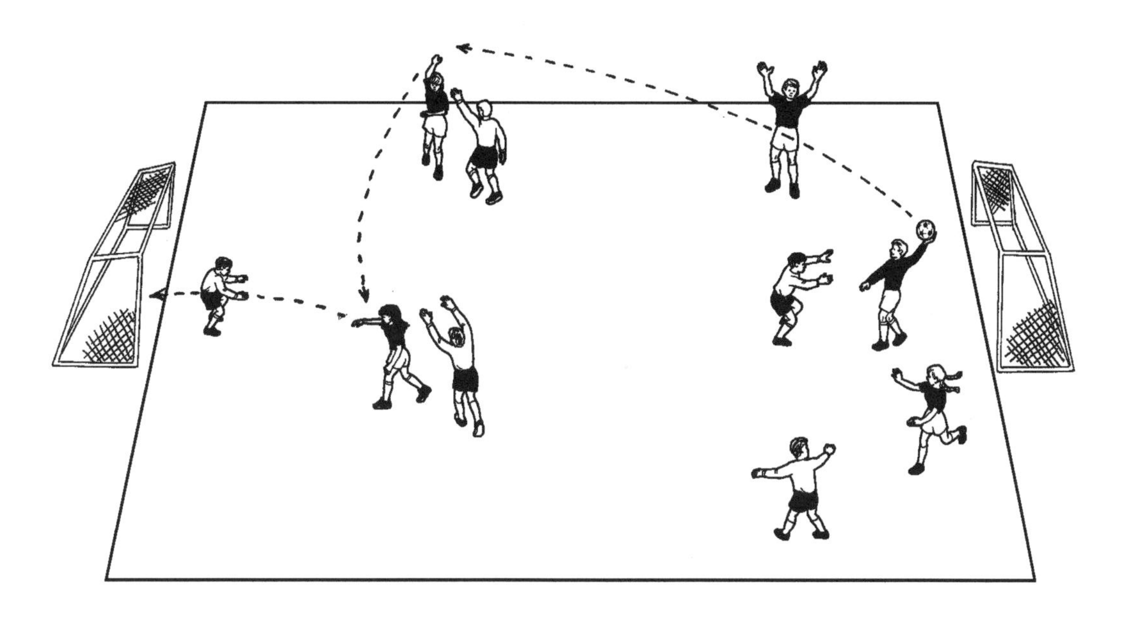

**Minutes:** 15

**Players:** 10 to 16 (2 equal-sized teams of 5 to 8)

**Objectives:** To simulate the support movement used in actual game situations; to physically condition players in a warm-up activity

**Setup:** Use markers to create a 40-yard by 60-yard field area with a small goal positioned at the midpoint of each endline. Organize two teams of equal number. Use colored vests to differentiate teams. You'll need one ball per game. No goalies.

**Procedure:** Each team defends a goal. Regular soccer rules apply, except that players pass by throwing (and catching) rather than kicking the ball. Players may take up to three steps with the ball before releasing it to a teammate or throwing it (shooting) at the goal. Change of possession occurs when the ball drops to the ground, a pass is intercepted, or a goal is scored. Players may not wrestle the ball from an opponent. Although there are no designated goalkeepers, all players are free to use their hands to block opponents' shots at goal.

**Scoring:** A goal is scored by throwing the ball into the opponent's goal. The team scoring the most goals wins the game.

**Practice tips:** Teammates should attack as one compact unit, positioning at the proper angle and distance of support in relation to the player with the ball.

# Part II

# Passing and Receiving Games

A successful soccer team can be characterized as 11 individuals playing as one unit. Passing and receiving skills form the vital thread that connects the individual parts of the team, the players, into a smoothly functioning whole that is greater than the sum of its parts. The ability to pass the ball accurately and at the correct pace is essential for successful attacking combinations. Equally important is the ability to receive and control balls arriving on the ground and through the air. All players, including the goalkeeper, should become competent in passing and receiving the ball under the game pressures of movement, physical and mental fatigue, and the determined challenge of opponents. As a general rule, players should pass the ball along the ground rather than through the air. Ground passes are easier to control and can be played with greater accuracy than lofted passes. Three basic techniques—inside of the foot, outside of the foot, and the instep—are employed for ground passes. Despite the obvious advantages of ground passes, certain situations dictate that the ball be played through the air. For example, an opponent might be blocking the passing lane between the player on the ball and a teammate stationed in a dangerous attacking position. Or a player might want to serve the ball to a teammate sprinting into open space behind the opponent's defense. In such situations the ball can be lofted (chipped) through the air.

Each passed ball should be received and controlled by a teammate. Ground balls are generally controlled with either the inside or outside surface of the foot. Balls taken directly out of the air can be received with the instep, thigh, chest, or, in rare instances, the head. In all cases, the player should withdraw the receiving surface as the ball arrives to cushion the impact and provide a soft target. A player's first touch of the passed ball as it arrives is the most important touch. Players who read the pressure correctly and control the ball into the space away from a challenging opponent afford themselves additional space and time to initiate their next movement. Conversely, players who touch the ball into pressure are more likely to lose possession. Proper positioning of the body as the ball is controlled is also important for maintaining possession, particularly when an opponent is trying to win the ball. Emphasize these points in all passing and receiving exercises.

The games in this section focus on the development of common passing and receiving techniques, although other soccer skills are rehearsed as well. The overriding objective of each game is for players to become more competent and confident in performing these skills. In short, players should become more comfortable on the ball. Modify the games to emphasize specific passing and receiving skills. You can also easily adapt them to accommodate the age, ability, and physical maturity of your players.

# 20 Touch, Turn, and Play On

**Minutes:** 12 minutes

**Players:** 12 to 18

**Objective:** To receive and turn the ball with the first touch

**Setup:** Split the team into three equal groups of four to six players each. Two groups combine to form a circle about 30 yards in diameter. The players (servers) forming the perimeter of the circle each have a ball. Players in the third group position themselves within the circle (without balls).

**Procedure:** Beginning at your command, players stationed within the circle move toward the perimeter to receive passes from the servers. Players receive and turn the ball with their first touch, then play it to a server who is without a ball. After turning and passing the ball, the middle player immediately checks toward another server to receive another ball. Players continue to receive, turn, and pass for as many repetitions as possible in two minutes, after which the players from one of the server groups move into the middle of the circle. The original middle group then positions on the perimeter as servers. Play several two-minute rounds with a different group in the middle for each round.

**Scoring:** Complete as many repetitions as you can in two minutes.

**Practice tips:** Players must check hard toward a server in order to receive and turn in one fluid motion. Passes need to be accurate and properly weighted.

# 21 First-Time Passing

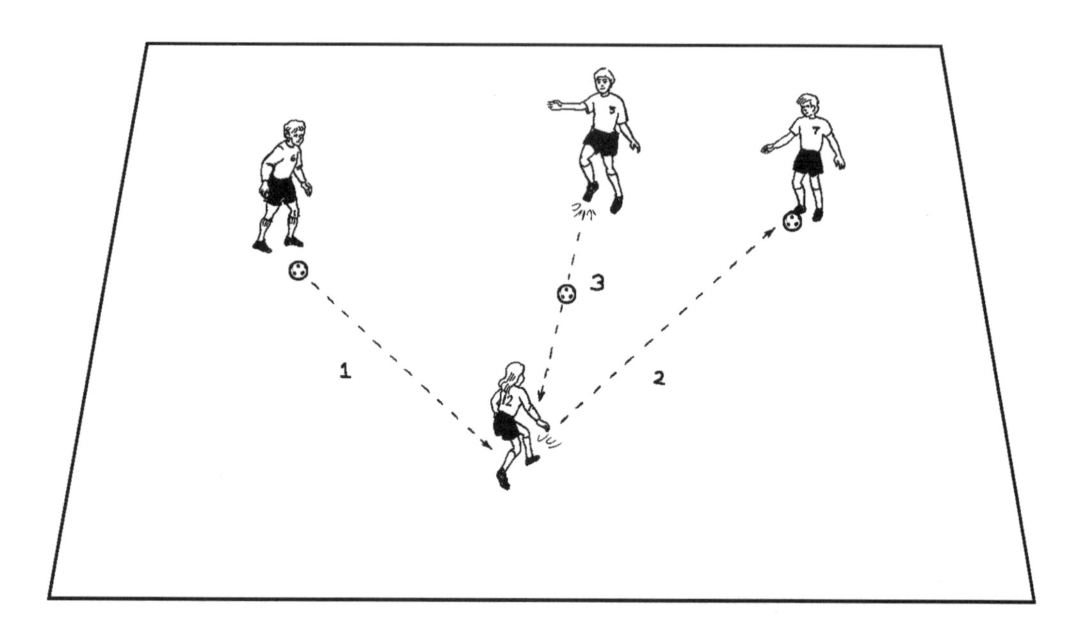


**Minutes:** 10

**Players:** Groups of 4

**Objective:** To play quick, accurate passes while maintaining proper body shape and balance

**Setup:** Three players (servers) position side by side two yards apart. The fourth player (target) faces the servers from a distance of five yards. Servers 1 and 2 each have a ball; server 3 does not have a ball to begin.

**Procedure:** Server 1 begins by passing the ball to the target, who returns it using a first-time, inside-of-the-foot pass to server 3. Server 2 immediately plays a ball to the target player, who returns it to server 1, who is without a ball. Continue the exercise at maximum speed for two minutes, after which one of the servers switches position with the target player. Repeat until each player has taken a turn as the target player.

**Scoring:** Perform as many repetitions as you can in two minutes.

**Practice tips:** Passes from servers must be accurate and properly weighted. If a ball goes astray, the game continues with the second ball, with no stop in play. The target player should square hips and shoulders with the server to whom he or she is passing.

**Variations:** The target player can pass the ball with the inside of the foot or the outside of the foot. Servers can pass the ball along the ground or use their hands to toss air balls to the target player, who must receive, control, and return the ball.

# 22 Tempo Passing

**Minutes:** 15

**Players:** Groups of 4

**Objectives:** To develop short-, medium-, and long-range passing skills; to introduce the concept of attacking support around the ball; to draw opponents to the vicinity of the ball and then change the point of attack

**Setup:** Organize players into groups of four, with one ball per group. Play in an area of at least 30 by 50 yards.

**Procedure:** Players interpass while moving throughout the field area, executing passing combinations in a short-short-long tempo sequence. For example, players must play two short (5 to 10 yards), or supporting, passes followed by a longer pass (20 to 30 yards) designed to change the point of attack. Another short-short-long sequence immediately follows. Short passes should be played on the ground; the long pass can be played on the ground or lofted through the air.

**Scoring:** None

**Practice tips:** Emphasize passing accuracy and proper pace. Perform the drill at game speed, even though there are no defenders applying pressure. Make the exercise more demanding by placing restrictions on players (such as limiting the number of touches allowed) or by adding the pressure of a defending opponent(s).

# 23 Fancy Footwork

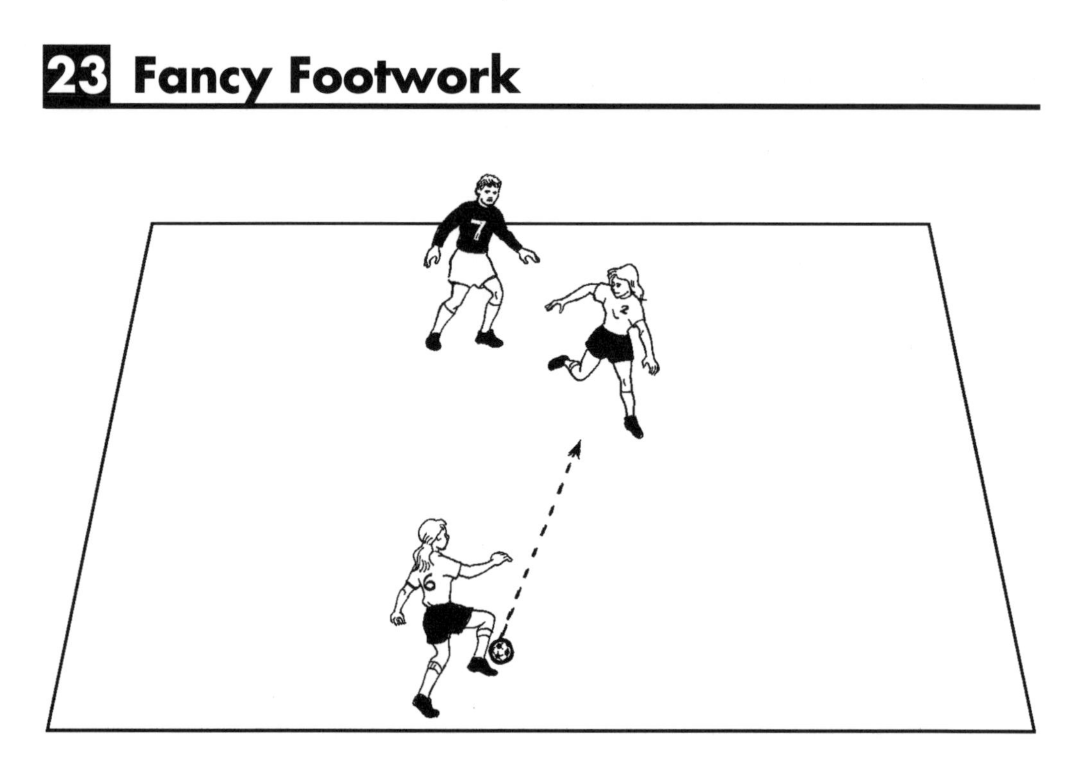

**Minutes:** 18 minutes (9 segments of 2 minutes each)

**Players:** Groups of 3

**Objectives:** To make accurate one-touch passes; to develop precise checking runs; to improve fitness

**Setup:** Players 1 and 2 position in single file about a yard apart. Player 3, with a ball, faces players 1 and 2 at a distance of 10 yards.

**Procedure:** Player 1 is the resting player for the first two-minute segment; player 2 is the working player; player 3 is the server. The exercise begins with player 2 sprinting forward past player 1. Player 3 passes the ball to player 2, who returns it with a one-touch pass. Player 2 immediately backpedals to his or her original position behind player 1, then sprints forward past player 1 (on the opposite side) to play a one-touch pass with the opposite foot. Player 2 continues the passing sequence, alternating passes with the right and left foot, at maximum speed for two minutes. All passes are made with the inside of the foot. After two minutes players rotate positions and repeat. Each player takes a total of three turns as the "working" player.

**Scoring:** Players complete as many one-touch passes as they can in two minutes.

**Practice tips:** Vary the type of pass (one-touch, two-touch, outside of the foot, and so on). Emphasize hard-checking runs toward the server and firm, crisp return passes.

# 24 Chip the Defender

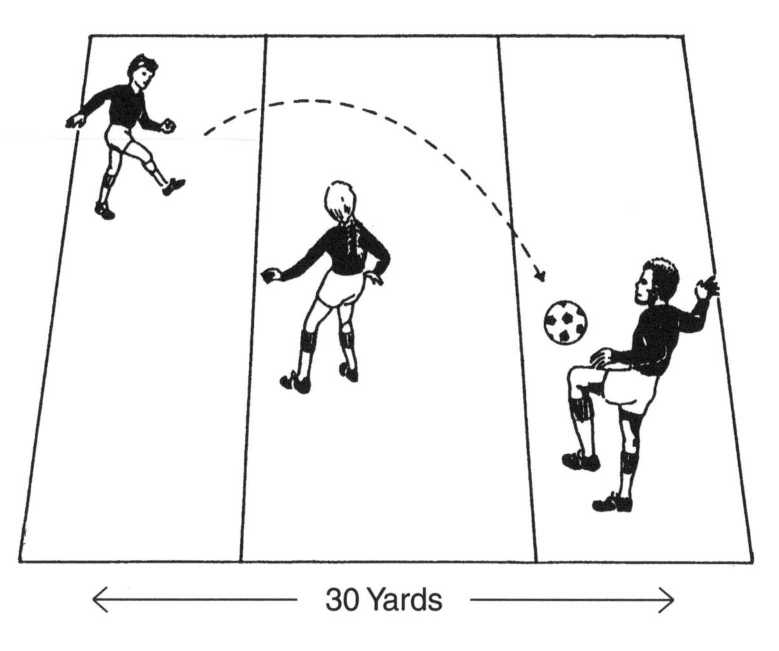


**Minutes:** 10 to 15

**Players:** Groups of 3

**Objective:** To chip the ball over a defender who is blocking the passing lane

**Setup:** Organize players into groups of three. Use markers to form a rectangular area 10 by 30 yards divided into three 10-yard by 10-yard zones for each group. Station one player in each zone. You'll need one ball per group.

**Procedure:** Players stationed in the end zones attempt to chip the ball back and forth over the player (defender) in the middle zone. Limit players to two touches. The first touch is used to control and prepare the ball, and the second to chip the defender. The defender tries to intercept passes by fronting the server and blocking the passing lane, but he or she may not leave the middle zone.

**Scoring:** Servers compete against the defender. Each chip pass over the defender that drops directly into the end zone counts as 2 points. End zone players are penalized 1 point if they use more than two touches to control and return the ball or if the ball leaves the playing area. The defender is awarded 1 point for each pass intercepted or blocked. Play to 20 points, then repeat, with players rotating into a different zone.

**Practice tips:** Chips must be high enough to clear defenders. Players should use a short, powerful kicking motion to drive the instep underneath the ball. This puts slight backspin on the ball, which makes it easier to receive and control. This game is not appropriate for young players or novices who lack either the strength or technical ability to serve the ball accurately over distance.

# 25 Toss, Cushion, and Catch

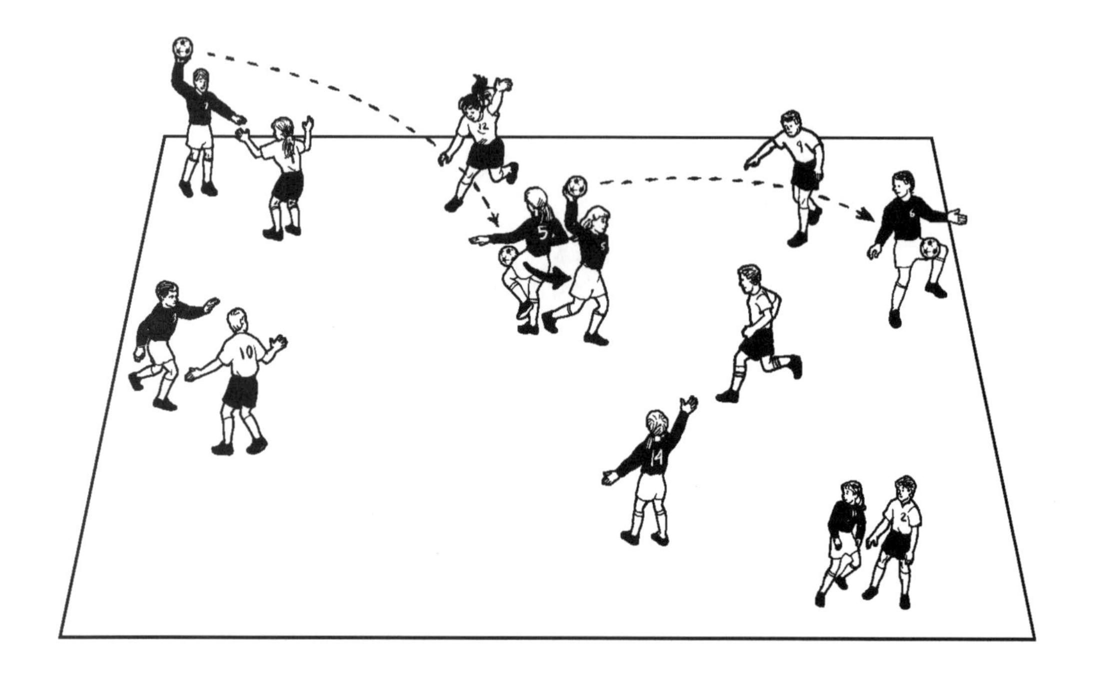

**Minutes:** 15

**Players:** 10 to 14 (2 teams of 5, 6, or 7)

**Objectives:** To receive and control balls dropping out of the air; to develop proper support angles for players in the vicinity of the ball; to improve endurance

**Setup:** Use markers to outline a playing area 30 by 40 yards. Organize the group into two teams of equal number and station both teams within the area. Use colored scrimmage vests to differentiate teams. Give one team the ball to begin.

**Procedure:** The team with the ball plays "keep away" from its opponents, throwing passes rather than kicking them. Players receive the ball using their instep, thigh, chest, or head and then catch it with their hands before it drops to the ground. Players may take up to five steps while in possession of the ball before passing to a teammate. The defending team gains possession of the ball by intercepting an opponent's pass or when an opponent fails to control the ball before it drops to the ground. Players can't wrestle the ball away from opponents.

**Scoring:** Award 1 team point for 10 consecutive passes. The team scoring the most points wins.

**Practice tips:** Players can provide a soft target by withdrawing the receiving surface (foot, thigh, etc. ) as the ball arrives to cushion the impact. Adjust the size of the area to accommodate the number of players. This game might not be appropriate for young players who have not mastered fundamental receiving skills.

# 26 Connect the Dots

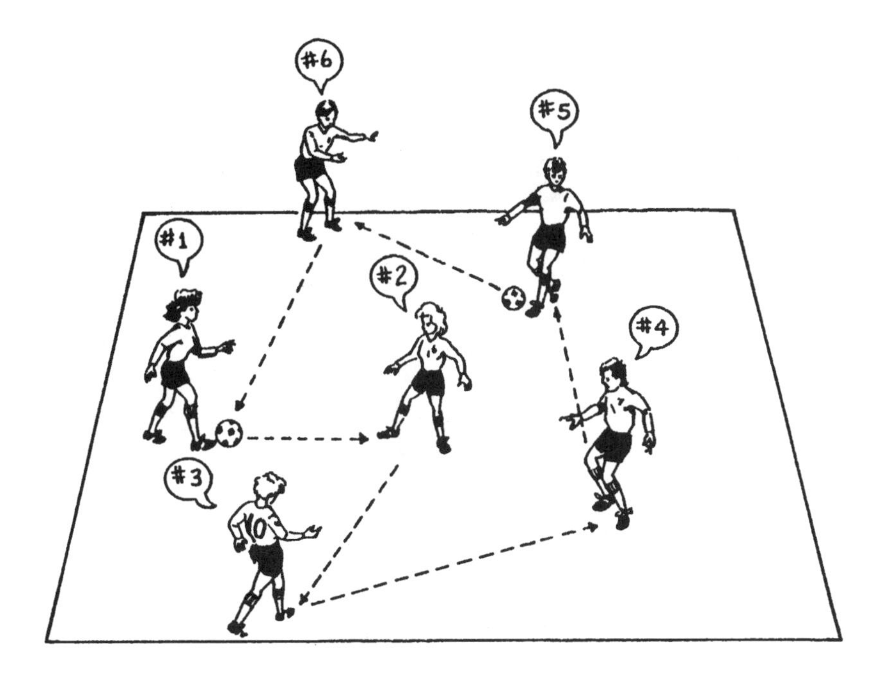


**Minutes:** 10 to 15

**Players:** Groups of 5 to 8

**Objectives:** To develop passing and receiving skills; to improve endurance

**Setup:** Use markers to outline a playing area 30 by 40 yards for each group. Players station within the area. Label each player with a number, beginning with 1 and continuing up through the number of players in the group. Two players each have a ball to begin.

**Procedure:** On your command, all players begin moving within the area. Those with a ball dribble; those without a ball position to make themselves available to receive a ball from the player numbered below him or her. All players move continuously during the exercise, passing to the teammate numbered above them and receiving passes from the teammate numbered below them. The highest number player passes to player 1 to complete the circuit.

**Scoring:** None

**Practice tips:** The game should flow continuously as players pass and receive the ball under control. Players should not stop the ball completely as they receive it. They should control the ball in the direction (space) of their next movement. Make the game more challenging by placing restrictions on players (such as having them pass with only their weakest foot or with only the outside or instep surface of the foot).

# 27 Soccer Dodge Ball

**Minutes:** 3 minutes per round or until all players are eliminated, whichever comes first

**Players:** 12 to 20 (2 equal-sized teams of 6 to 10)

**Objectives:** To improve passing and dribbling skills; to develop agility, mobility, and fitness

**Setup:** Use markers to outline a playing area 25 by 35 yards. Team A stations within the area without soccer balls. Team B stations outside the area, each player with a ball.

**Procedure:** At your command, Team B players dribble into the area and attempt to pass their balls to contact Team A players below the knees. All passes must be made with the inside or outside surface of the foot. Team A players are free to move anywhere within the area to avoid being hit by a ball. Any player contacted with a ball below the knees is eliminated from the game. That player must go outside the area and practice individual ball juggling until the game is completed. The game continues for three minutes or until all Team A players have been eliminated, whichever comes first. Repeat with Team B stationed within the area without soccer balls.

**Scoring:** You be the official timekeeper. The team eliminating all its opponents in the least amount of time wins. Repeat the game several times, switching team roles each time.

**Practice tips:** Emphasize passing accuracy rather than power. Encourage players to dribble as close as they can to their intended target before passing the ball. Adjust the playing area size to accommodate the ages and abilities of your players.

# 28 Hunt the Rabbit

**Minutes:** 15 (or 10 points, whichever comes first)

**Players:** Unlimited (3 teams of equal size)

**Objectives:** To develop passing skills; to improve general endurance

**Setup:** Use markers to outline a playing area 30 by 40 yards. Station three teams in the playing area. Use colored scrimmage vests to differentiate teams. Designate one player on each team as the "rabbit," who wears a distinctive shirt or hat. Each team has two soccer balls; six balls are in play at all times.

**Procedure:** The objective is to contact an opposing team's "rabbit" below the knees with a passed ball. Players move the ball into position to contact a rabbit through combination passing with teammates. Rabbits are free to move anywhere within the field area to avoid getting hit with a ball.

**Scoring:** A pass that contacts a rabbit below the knees scores 1 point for the team. Each team keeps total of its points scored. The first team to total 10 points (or the team with the highest number of points after 15 minutes) wins.

**Practice tips:** Reduce the area size for younger, less skilled players.

## 29 Moving Targets

**Minutes:** 15 to 20

**Players:** 12 to 16 (2 equal-sized teams of 6 to 8)

**Objective:** To coordinate team play through effective passing combinations, proper support movement, and purposeful off-the-ball running

**Setup:** Play on half a regulation field. Designate a player on each team to be the target player, who wears a distinctive colored vest or a hat. Use colored scrimmage vests to differentiate teams. Award one team possession of the ball.

**Procedure:** Teams have two primary goals: (1) to maintain possession of the ball from their opponents and (2) to complete passes to their target player. Targets should move constantly to make themselves available for passes from teammates. Change of possession occurs when a defending player intercepts a pass, when the ball travels out of the area, or after a pass is completed to a target. Regular soccer rules apply except that the offside rule is waived.

**Scoring:** Award 1 team point for six consecutive passes without loss of possession; award 2 points for a pass completed to a "target" player. The team scoring the most points wins.

**Practice tips:** Reduce the area for highly skilled players. For variations, designate two target players for each team or impose touch restrictions (such as two-touch passes only) or both.

# 30 Perimeter Passing

**Minutes:** 24

**Players:** 9 or 12 (3 teams of 3 or 4)

**Objectives:** To coordinate group passing combinations; to rehearse proper support movement; to execute the defensive principles of pressure, cover, and balance

**Setup:** Use markers to outline a field area of approximately 30 by 40 yards. Station one team within the area as defenders. The remaining teams position their players (attackers) along the perimeter of the area. You'll need one ball per game.

**Procedure:** Attackers attempt to keep the ball away from the outnumbered defenders. Attackers are allowed to move laterally along the perimeter lines to support their teammates or receive passes, but they may not enter the area. Attackers are limited to three or fewer touches to receive, control, and pass the ball. Defending players, being outnumbered, work together to close the attacking space and win the ball. A defending player who steals the ball returns it immediately to an attacker, and play continues. Play for eight minutes, then replay the game with a different team as defenders. Play a total of three games. Each team plays one eight-minute period as defenders.

**Scoring:** The defending team scores 1 point each time it gains possession or forces the attacking team to play the ball outside the playing area. The attacking teams score 1 point for eight consecutive passes. The highest point total wins.

**Practice tips:** Defending players work together to limit the attackers' options and eliminate passing lanes. Attacking players counter such tactics by quickly changing the point of attack (location of the ball) to prevent defenders from closing down the space. Adjust the playing area size to accommodate the ages and abilities of your players. The smaller the area, the easier the activity is for the defending team.

# 31 Four Versus Four Versus Four

**Minutes:** 15 to 20

**Players:** 12 (3 teams of 4)

**Objective:** To execute passing skills under game-simulated pressures

**Setup:** Play within the penalty area (44 by 18 yards). Differentiate groups by having them wear colored scrimmage vests. Designate one group as defenders. The two remaining groups combine to form an eight-player attacking team. The attacking team has the ball to begin.

**Procedure:** The eight-player team attempts to keep the ball away from the four-player team. Attackers are limited to two touches to receive and pass the ball. Change of possession occurs when a defending player steals the ball, when an attacker plays the ball out of the area, or when an attacker uses more than two touches to control the ball. The group of four whose player causes the loss of possession immediately becomes defenders, and the original defending team becomes attackers. Play continues as teams alternate from attack to defense.

**Scoring:** 10 passes in succession without loss of possession equals one goal.

**Practice tips:** Impose restrictions depending on the age and ability of players. For example, allow younger players three touches to control the ball, and restrict elite players to one-touch soccer. You might also increase the number of players to play 10 v 5 or 12 v 6, which reduces the space and time available to players when receiving and passing the ball.

# 32 Total Team Possession

**Minutes:** 15

**Players:** 15 to 21 (2 teams of 6 to 9; 3 neutral players)

**Objective:** To develop large-group passing combinations

**Setup:** Play on half a regulation field. Designate three players to be neutral, and organize remaining players into two teams of equal number. Use colored vests to differentiate the two teams and the neutral players. You'll need at least one soccer ball, but it's better to have more. Award one team possession of the ball to begin.

**Procedure:** The team with the ball tries to keep the ball away from its opponents. Neutral players combine with the team in possession to create a three-player advantage for the attacking team. Players, including the neutrals, are allowed three or fewer touches to pass and receive the ball. Teams reverse roles immediately upon change of possession, constantly switching from attack to defense and vice versa.

**Scoring:** Eight consecutive passes without losing possession earns 1 point. The team scoring the most points wins.

**Practice tips:** Emphasize basic principles of team play. The team in possession should stretch the field vertically and horizontally to create greater space and more time in which to receive and pass the ball. Defending players should work together to pressure the ball and compact the available space around the ball.

# 33 Play to the End Zones

**Minutes:** 20 to 25

**Players:** 6 to 10 (2 teams of 3, 4, or 5)

**Objective:** To improve players' ability to attack and defend within small groups

**Setup:** Use markers to outline a field area 50 by 25 yards. Designate a zone 10 yards deep at each end, spanning the width of the field. Assign each team an end zone to defend. Station both teams in the central area of the field between the end zones. No goals or goalkeepers are necessary. Award one team the ball to begin.

**Procedure:** Play begins with a kickoff from the center of the field. Basic soccer rules apply (other than the method of scoring). The team with the ball scores 1 point by completing a pass to a player who has moved into the opponent's end zone. Defending players may not enter their own end zone to intercept passes—they must collectively position to block passing lanes to prevent passes from entering their end zone. Change of possession occurs when the defending team steals the ball, when the ball goes out of play last touched by a member of the attacking team, or after each point scored. Otherwise, play is continuous.

**Scoring:** The attacking team is awarded 1 point for a completed pass received and controlled within the opponent's end zone. The team scoring the most points wins.

**Practice tips:** Adjust the field size to accommodate the ages and abilities of your players. Smaller end zones make it more difficult to score points, while larger (deeper and wider) end zones make it more difficult for defending players to prevent scores. Place restrictions on players to emphasize specific aspects of play (for example, discourage excessive dribbling by limiting players to three or fewer touches of the ball before passing).

# 34 Multiple Goals

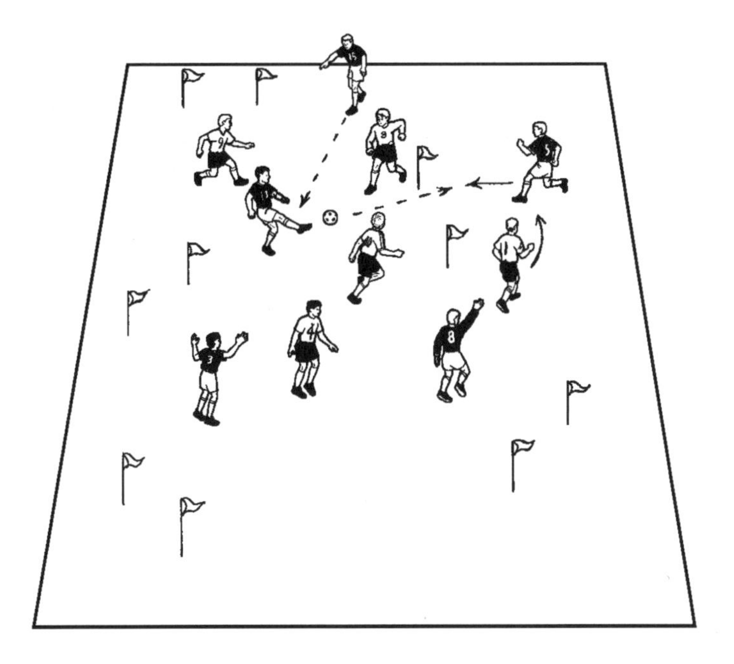

**Minutes:** 20

**Players:** 8 to 14 (2 equal-sized teams of 4 to 7)

**Objectives:** To develop passing and receiving skills; to improve one-on-one marking; to develop aerobic endurance

**Setup:** Play between the penalty areas of a regulation field. Position cones or flags to form five goals (three yards wide) randomly positioned within the area. Use colored vests to differentiate teams. You'll need one ball. Do not use goalkeepers.

**Procedure:** Award one team possession of the ball to begin. Teams can score in all five goals and must defend all five goals. Players score by completing a pass through a goal to a teammate stationed on the opposite side. The ball may be passed through either side of a goal but not twice consecutively through the same goal. Play is continuous. Change of possession occurs when the defending team steals the ball or when the ball leaves the playing area last touched by the attacking team. Change of possession does not occur after each goal. Regular soccer rules apply, except that the offside rule is waived.

**Scoring:** Teams score 1 point for each pass through a goal to a teammate. The team scoring the most points wins.

**Practice tips:** Prohibiting consecutive scores through the same goal encourages players to switch the point of attack to penetrate the goal area with the fewest opponents. Require one-on-one marking to reduce the space and time available for players to pass and receive the ball.

# 35 Soccer Volleyball

**Minutes:** 20

**Players:** 8 to 16 (2 equal-sized teams of 4 to 8)

**Objective:** To receive and control balls dropping out of the air

**Setup:** Play on an outdoor volleyball court, if available. If not, use markers to form a rectangular area 20 by 40 yards. Stretch a net or rope about six feet high across the center of the court. Station one team on each side of the net. You'll need one soccer ball. Award one team the serve to begin.

**Procedure:** Players may use their head or feet to play the ball. The server positions behind the endline. The ball must be chipped (off the ground) over the net and land within the opponent's court to constitute a good serve. The ball may bounce once before it's returned, although it's also okay to return the serve with a first-time volley. (This applies to all plays, not only service returns.) Teammates are allowed to pass to one another in the air before returning the ball over the net. A fault occurs if

- the serve or return fails to clear the net,
- the serve or return lands out of bounds,
- the ball bounces more than once, or
- a player uses arms or hands to pass or control the ball.

If the serving team commits a fault, it loses the serve to opponents.

**Scoring:** Only the serving team scores points. The serving team earns 1 point for each fault by the receiving team. The first team to score 21 points wins. Play three games.

**Practice tips:** Soccer volleyball is a good choice for the day after a match, when players are physically tired and have sore muscles. This game is not appropriate for younger players who lack the skill or physical maturity to serve and receive the ball out of the air.

# Part III

# Dribbling, Shielding, and Tackling Games

Dribbling in soccer serves much the same function as dribbling in basketball—it enables a player to maintain possession of the ball while running past opponents. Effective dribbling skills used in appropriate situations can break down a defense and are vital to a team's attack. On the flip side, excessive dribbling in inappropriate areas of the field might hinder or disrupt the team play necessary to create quality goal-scoring opportunities. Players must be schooled to recognize when and where to dribble and to respond accordingly. In general, dribbling skills are used to best advantage in the attacking third of the field nearest the opponent's goal. A player who can successfully take on (dribble past) an opponent in that area has created a potential scoring opportunity—or at least a situation that can lead to a scoring opportunity. Less dribbling should be done in the middle and defending thirds of the field, areas where the potential penalty (i.e., a goal against) for possession loss is greater than the potential reward of beating an opponent on the dribble.

Two general dribbling styles are employed in game situations. Players use short, choppy steps and sudden changes of speed and direction when dribbling in tight spaces. In such situations, eluding defenders and protecting the ball are of paramount importance. When players run with the ball in open space, ball protection is less important than moving the ball at speed. In open space, players push the ball forward several steps with the outside surface of the instep, sprint to the ball, and then push it again.

There's no single best technique to use to dribble the ball. Players should develop their own dribbling style that achieves the primary objective of beating an opponent while maintaining possession of the ball. Granted, key elements such as close control of the ball, deceptive body feints, and sudden changes of speed and direction are common to all successful dribbling styles. The ways in which players incorporate such maneuvers into their dribbling style can vary, however. In essence, if a style works for a player, that style is right for the player.

Shielding skills are often used in conjunction with dribbling skills to protect the ball from an opponent challenging for possession. The player with the ball positions her body between the ball and the opponent attempting to steal it. The ball is controlled with the foot farthest from the opponent, and the dribbler readjusts position in response to pressure from the opponent. This technique is called "screening" the ball.

Tackling is strictly a defensive skill used to steal the ball from an opponent. Three different techniques—the block tackle, poke tackle, and slide tackle—are used, depending on the situation. The block tackle is used when an opponent is dribbling directly at a defender. The poke and slide tackles are used when a defender is approaching the dribbler from the side or from behind. The block tackle has advantages over the poke and slide tackles. The block allows for greater body control and enables the defender to initiate an immediate counterattack once the ball has been won. In addition, if the player fails to win the ball, he is still in position to recover and chase after the opponent.

The practice games in this section emphasize the development of dribbling, shielding, and tackling skills, often within the same game. Most of the exercises also involve a degree of fitness training because players are moving continuously.

# 36 Shadow Dribble

**Minutes:** 10

**Players:** Unlimited (in pairs)

**Objective:** To improve dribbling skills through the use of subtle body feints, sudden changes of speed and direction, and deceptive foot movements

**Setup:** Pair each player with a partner. Play on half a regulation field, one ball per player.

**Procedure:** Partners dribble randomly throughout the area, one leading while the other closely follows. The trailing player attempts to mimic, or shadow, the movements of the leader. Partners change positions every 45 to 60 seconds.

**Scoring:** None

**Practice tips:** Players should keep their heads up while dribbling to maximize their field of vision. Emphasize fluid and controlled movement with the ball. Make the exercise more challenging by requiring players to increase their dribbling speed or by reducing the playing area so that players must keep close control of the ball within a confined space.

# 37 Soccer Marbles

**Minutes:** 12

**Players:** Unlimited (in groups of 3)

**Objective:** To develop dribbling and shielding skills

**Setup:** Use markers to outline a 20-by 30-yard playing area for each group. Three players, each with a ball, position on the perimeter of the area. One player is "it," and the others are chasers.

**Procedure:** The player who is "it" dribbles into the area. The chasers follow closely and attempt to pass and contact the "it" player's ball with their own. The "it" player attempts to elude the chasers by executing sudden changes of speed and direction while maintaining close control of the ball. Play for two minutes, after which players take a brief rest. Players then switch roles and repeat the game. Continue until each player has taken two turns being "it."

**Scoring:** The "it" player is assessed 1 penalty point each time his or her ball is contacted by one of the chaser's balls. The player with the fewest penalty points at the end of the game wins.

**Practice tips:** Make the game more challenging by adding an additional chaser to the game or reducing the size of the playing area.

# 38 Cone to Cone

**Minutes:** 12 to 18 (in 60- to 90-second periods)

**Players:** Unlimited (in pairs)

**Objectives:** To develop deceptive foot movements and body feints used to unbalance an opponent; to improve mobility and agility; to develop aerobic endurance

**Setup:** Place two markers 10 to 12 yards apart on the sideline or endline of the field. Partners face one another on opposite sides of the line, between the markers. One player (attacker) has the ball, and the other plays as the defender.

**Procedure:** Neither player may cross the line that separates them. The attacker attempts to dribble laterally to either marker before the defender can position there. Play continuously for 90 seconds. After a short rest, players exchange possession of the ball and repeat. Play six rounds.

**Scoring:** The attacker scores 1 point each time he or she beats the defender to a marker with the ball under control. The player who scores the most points wins the game.

**Practice tips:** Combine deceptive body movements with sudden changes of speed and direction to unbalance the defender. Make the game more physically demanding by increasing the distance between cones to 15 yards. As a variation, organize a tournament with winners advancing to play different opponents.

# 39 Speed Dribble Relay

**Minutes:** 10

**Players:** Unlimited (in pairs)

**Objectives:** To improve dribbling speed; to develop aerobic endurance

**Setup:** Play on a regulation field. Use the front edge of one penalty area as the starting line and the halfway line as the turn-around line. Players pair off and station along the starting line, with one ball per pair.

**Procedure:** On your call of "Go!" one member of each pair dribbles at maximum speed to the halfway line, turns, dribbles back to the starting line, and exchanges possession of the ball with his or her partner, who in turn dribbles the circuit at top speed.

**Scoring:** The first pair to complete the circuit (penalty area to halfway line and back to penalty area) wins the race. Run at least 10 races, with short rests between each.

**Practice tips:** The technique used when dribbling at speed differs from that used when dribbling for close control. Rather than keeping the ball close to their feet, players use the outside surface of the foot to push the ball two or three yards ahead and sprint to it. Adjust the race distance to accommodate the ages and abilities of your players. Shorten the distance for players 10 years old and under.

# 40 Slalom Dribbling Race

**Minutes:** 10 to 15

**Players:** Unlimited (groups of 3 to 5)

**Objectives:** To improve dribbling speed and control; to improve fitness

**Setup:** Teammates line up in single file facing a line of 6 to 10 markers. Allow three to four yards between markers. Each team needs one ball.

**Procedure:** On your call of "Go!" the first player in each line dribbles as quickly as possible through the slalom course, weaving in and out of the markers front to back to front. On returning to the starting line, the dribbler exchanges the ball with the next player in line, who repeats the circuit. Teammates dribble the course in turn. The team whose players complete the course first wins the race. Repeat the race several times, with a short rest between each.

**Scoring:** Teams get 10 points for winning a race, 8 points for second place, and 6 points for third place. Penalize players 1 team point for each marker bypassed or knocked over. Determine team point totals by subtracting the total number of penalty points from points awarded for the team's order of finish in the race. The first team to 50 points wins the event.

**Practice tips:** To make the game more difficult, reduce the distance between markers or increase the number of markers.

# 41 Takeover

**Minutes:** 5 to 10

**Players:** Unlimited (entire team)

**Objective:** To execute a takeover maneuver (possession exchange) with a teammate

**Setup:** Use markers to form a rectangular area 25 by 30 yards. All players position within the area, with one ball for every two players.

**Procedure:** All players move randomly throughout the playing area. Those with a ball dribble, those without a ball jog at half- to three-quarter speed. Dribblers look to exchange possession of the ball with one of the free players, using the "takeover" maneuver.

**Scoring:** None

**Practice tips:** Players communicate with each other through verbal signals or subtle body movements. When executing the takeover, the player dribbling the ball should control it with the foot farthest from an imaginary defender. To make the game more difficult, add one or two passive defenders to the exercise.

# 42 Wolves and Sheep

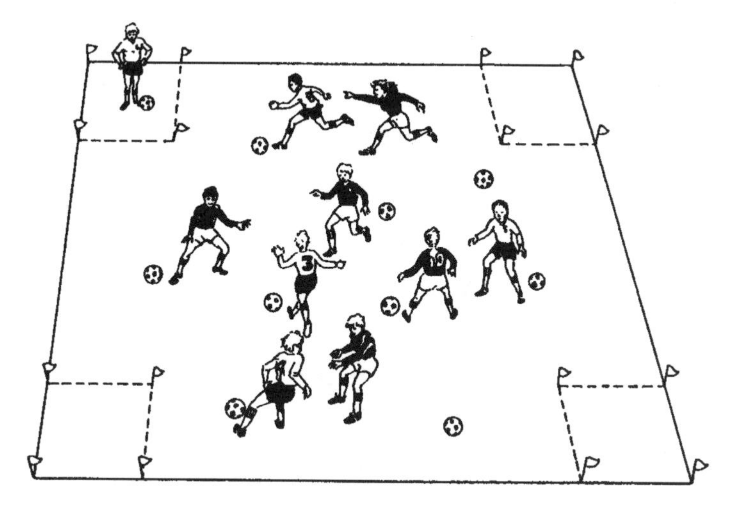

**Minutes:** 10 to 15

**Players:** Unlimited (2 equal-sized teams)

**Objectives:** To improve dribbling speed and control; to develop individual defending skills

**Setup:** Use markers to outline a 40- by 40-yard square. The size of the area may vary depending on the number of players involved. Mark off a safety zone (five yards square) in each corner of the field area. Organize two teams of equal numbers, assigning a name to each team (such as Blues and Reds). Use colored vests to differentiate teams. All players station within the area, each with a ball.

**Procedure:** At your command, players of both teams dribble randomly among themselves within the area (avoiding the safety zones) while maintaining close control of the ball. After a few seconds, shout out one of the team names (such as, "Blues!"), at which point all that team's players attempt to dribble into a safety zone, but with one restriction: they can't dribble into the safety zone closest to them. The second team's players leave their balls and attempt to tag the first team's players (with a hand) before they reach a safety zone. The chasers are the "wolves" while the players attempting to dribble into a safety zone are the "sheep." Sheep are safe once they enter a safety zone. The round ends when all the first team's players have been tagged or have dribbled into a safety zone. At this point, players from both teams return to the center of the area and restart the game for round 2. Play several rounds, with teams alternating as wolves and sheep at your discretion.

**Scoring:** Sheep who reach a safety zone before being tagged score 1 team point. The team scoring the most points after several repetitions of the game wins.

**Practice tips:** For advanced players, enlarge the playing area or require wolves to dribble a ball while giving chase.

# 43 Penetrate a Layered Defense

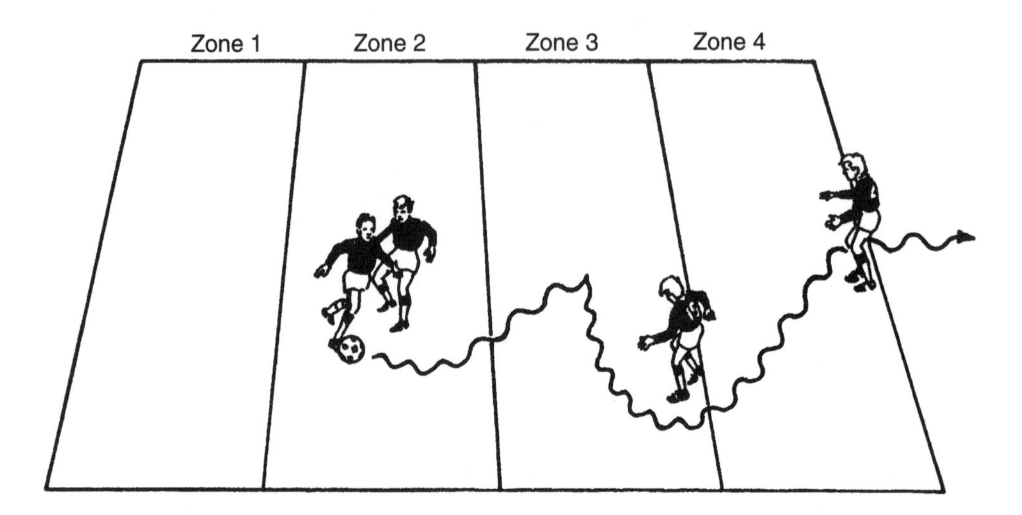


**Minutes:** 10 to 15

**Players:** Groups of 4

**Objectives:** To take on and beat a defender; to improve individual defending skills

**Setup:** Use markers to form a 10- by 40-yard area for each group of four, divided into four equal zones 10 by 10 yards. Position one player in each zone. The player (attacker) in zone 1 has the ball and faces the other three players (defenders).

**Procedure:** The attacker tries to dribble past the defenders stationed in zones 2, 3, and 4. Defenders are restricted to their assigned zone. If an attacker dribbles past a defender in one zone, he or she continues forward to take on the player in the next zone. A defender who steals the ball immediately returns it to the attacker so that the attacker can continue to advance to take on the defender in the next zone. After taking on the defender in zone 4, the attacker remains in that zone to play as a defender in the next round. Each of the original defenders moves forward one zone. The player who moves into zone 1 becomes the attacker for round 2. Repeat until each player has taken five turns as the attacker.

**Scoring:** Attackers score 1 point for each defender they beat on the dribble. The player who totals the most points after five turns as an attacker wins.

**Practice tips:** Station defenders on the back line of their respective zones. From this position, they can move forward to challenge once the attacker enters their area. Prohibit slide tackles.

# 44 Tackle All Balls

**Minutes:** 10 to 15

**Players:** 10 to 18

**Objectives:** To improve individual defending; to develop dribbling and shielding skills; to improve fitness

**Setup:** Use markers to form a rectangular area about 25 by 35 yards. Designate two players as defenders, who position without balls outside the area. Remaining players, each with a ball, station in the area.

**Procedure:** Players dribble randomly within the area. On your command, defenders enter the area to give chase and gain possession of a ball. Players who lose their ball to a defender immediately become defenders and attempt to steal someone else's ball. The defender gaining possession of a ball keeps it and becomes a dribbler (attacker). Play is continuous as players alternate playing as defenders and attackers.

**Scoring:** None

**Practice tips:** Have players use either block or poke tackles to dispossess a dribbler. Prohibit slide tackles because of the crowded conditions. Designate additional defenders to make the game more challenging for the dribblers.

# 45 Too Few Balls

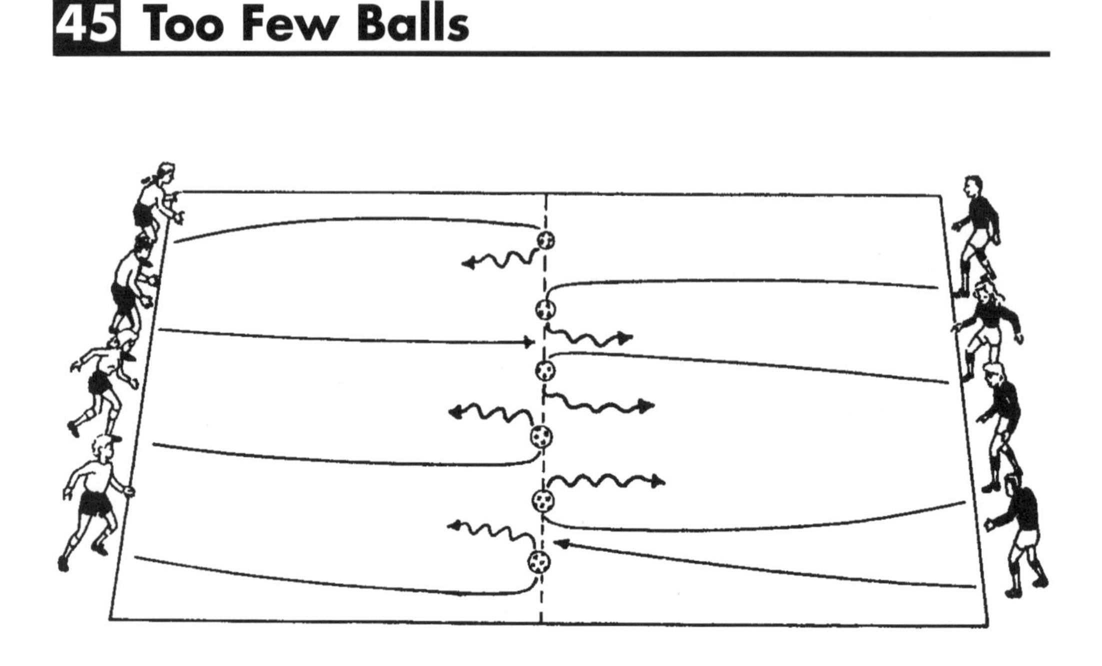

**Minutes:** 10 to 15

**Players:** 8 to 16 (2 equal-sized teams of 4 to 8)

**Objectives:** To improve dribbling speed; to develop aerobic endurance

**Setup:** Use markers to form a rectangular area 30 by 50 yards divided lengthwise by a midline. Organize two teams of equal number. Station teams on opposite endlines, with players an equal distance apart facing the center of the field. Place a supply of balls evenly spaced along the midline (use two fewer balls than the number of players involved). Use colored vests to differentiate teams.

**Procedure:** On your command of "Go!" players from both teams sprint to the midline, compete for possession of a ball, and attempt to return it over their own endline by dribbling. Because there are two fewer balls than players, the two players who do not immediately secure a ball must chase after opponents and prevent them from returning their balls over the endline by kicking the balls out of the field area. The round ends when all balls have been returned over an endline or played out of the field area. Reposition all balls on the midline and repeat the activity. Play at least 10 rounds.

**Scoring:** Teams get 1 point for each ball returned over its endline. A ball must be dribbled under control over an endline to count as a point scored. The team scoring the most points after 10 rounds wins.

**Practice tips:** Don't allow slide tackles, particularly those initiated from behind.

# 46 All Versus All

**Minutes:** 10 to 15

**Players:** 10 to 20

**Objectives:** To develop dribbling, shielding, and tackling skills; to improve fitness

**Setup:** Use markers to form a rectangular area about 25 by 30 yards. All players station within the playing area, each with a ball.

**Procedure:** To begin, players dribble randomly within the area, avoiding all other players. On a signal from you, the exercise becomes "All Versus All." Each player attempts to kick other players' balls out of the area while maintaining possession of his or her own ball. A player whose ball is kicked out of the area is eliminated from the game. Eliminated players retrieve their ball and practice ball juggling to the side of the field area. The game continues until only one player remains in possession of his or her ball. Repeat the activity several times.

**Scoring:** None

**Practice tips:** Vary the size of the area depending on the number of players. Require players to use either the block or poke tackle when attempting to steal a teammate's ball. Don't allow slide tackles because of the crowded conditions.

# 47 Streak to Goal

**Minutes:** 10-15

**Players:** 10 to 16 (2 equal-sized teams of 5 to 8)

**Objectives:** To improve dribbling speed; to develop general endurance

**Setup:** Play on a regulation field. Organize two teams of equal numbers and give each a name, such as "Strikers" and "Kickers." Players from both teams, each with a ball, station within the center circle of the field. Each team defends an endline of the field. Use colored vests to differentiate teams. No goals or goalkeepers necessary.

**Procedure:** To begin, players from both teams dribble randomly within the center circle. After 10 to 15 seconds, shout a team name, such as "Strikers!" All Striker players immediately leave the circle to dribble at top speed toward the Kickers' endline. Kickers leave their balls and give chase, attempting to catch and dispossess Striker players before they can dribble their balls over the endline. A Kicker who steals a ball dribbles it back into the center circle. The round ends when all balls have been dribbled over the endline or returned into the center circle. Play 8 to 10 rounds, alternating teams from attacking to defending.

**Scoring:** The attacking team scores 1 point for each ball dribbled over an endline. The defending team scores 1 point for each ball stolen and dribbled back to the center circle. The team scoring the most points wins.

**Practice tips:** Adjust the field size to accommodate the age and abilities of your players. Younger players (12 and under) use a three-quarter field. Defending players should take the most direct recovery to a point between the endline and the opponent they are tracking down. Once goal side, defenders can challenge for the ball. Don't allow slide tackles from behind.

# Part IV

# Heading and Shooting Games

Heading and shooting skills are used to put the finishing touch on a successful attack. This is easier said than done, because scoring goals remains the single most difficult task in soccer. During the 2002 World Cup, tournament players such as Ronaldo of Brazil, Raul of Spain, and Michael Owen of England received most of the media attention—and rightly so. These players and a handful of others make up a select group of world-class scorers. They are the ultimate marksmen of international soccer. Although a goal scored is generally the result of a team effort, the player who can consistently finish the attack by putting the ball in the back of the net is a rare and valuable team member.

Success as a goal scorer depends on several factors, one of which is the ability to shoot with power and accuracy. Intangibles such as determination, anticipation, confidence, composure under pressure, and a burning desire to score also factor into the equation. Players might use several different shooting techniques during the course of a game, depending on whether the ball is rolling, bouncing, or taken directly out of the air. The instep drive is used to strike a rolling or stationary ball. The full volley, half-volley, and side volley are used to strike a bouncing ball or a ball that's dropping from above.

Soccer is the only sport in which players literally use their heads to propel the ball. Scoring opportunities can originate from balls crossed from the flank, corner kicks, free kicks, and long throw-ins. A player uses the *jump header* technique when leaping above an opponent who is also trying to head the ball. The player uses a two-footed takeoff to jump up, arches his upper body back, and then snaps forward at the waist to contact the ball on the flat surface of the forehead. During an attempt to score, the ball should be driven on a downward plane toward the goal line. The *dive header* technique is an acrobatic skill used to score off a low-driven cross traveling across the goal area. The player dives parallel to the ground with the head held firm and tilted back. Contact is on the flat surface of the forehead, with arms and hands extended downward to break the fall to the ground.

The heading and shooting games in this section expose your players to the competitive pressures they'll face in game situations—pressures such as restricted space, limited time, physical fatigue, and determined opponents. Modify the exercises to emphasize the scoring technique of your choice. You can also easily adapt the exercises to make them more or less difficult by adjusting variables such as area size, number of touches permitted, and number of players participating.

# 48 Toss-Head-Score

**Minutes:** 10

**Players:** Unlimited (groups of 3)

**Objective:** To develop the heading technique used to score goals

**Setup:** Use markers to form an area 10 by 15 yards for each group. Position flags or cones to represent a goal four yards wide on one end of the area. Station one player in the goal to play goalkeeper, one player to the side of the goal to be server, and one player eight yards front and center of the goal as the "header." You'll need one ball.

**Procedure:** The server tosses the ball upward so that it drops near the center of the area. The header judges the ball's flight, moves forward, and attempts to score by heading the ball past the goalkeeper. Players rotate positions after each attempt on goal and repeat the activity. Play for 10 minutes continuous.

**Scoring:** Award 2 points for a goal scored and 1 point for a header on goal saved by the keeper. The player who has scored the most points at the completion of the exercise wins.

**Practice tips:** Players should head the ball downward toward a corner of the goal. Emphasize proper heading form (upper body arched back from the vertical, chin tucked, neck stiff, ball contacted on forehead). Allow beginning players to head the ball with both feet on the ground; require advanced players to jump and head the ball.

# 49 Jack in the Box

**Minutes:** 10

**Players:** Unlimited (groups of 3)

**Objectives:** To improve jump header technique and timing; to develop leg strength and endurance

**Setup:** Three players position in line 10 yards apart. The third player positions midway between the end players (servers 1 and 2). Each server has a ball.

**Procedure:** Server 1 tosses a ball upward toward the middle player, who jumps and heads the ball directly back to the server. The middle player immediately turns 180 degrees to jump and head a ball tossed by server 2. Continue at maximum speed for 30 headers, after which the middle player exchanges places with one of the servers. Repeat the exercise until each player has taken a minimum of two turns in the middle.

**Scoring:** Award 1 point for each ball headed directly back to the server's chest. The player scoring the most points wins.

**Practice tips:** Players should jump vertically upward (not forward), arch their upper trunk back prior to the ball's arrival, and then snap forward to contact the ball with their forehead. They should keep the head steady with eyes open and mouth closed on contact with the ball.

# 50 Heading Goal to Goal

**Minutes:** 15

**Players:** Unlimited (in pairs)

**Objective:** To develop jump header technique

**Setup:** Players (1 and 2) pair up for heading competition. Use markers to form a rectangular area 10 by 12 yards for each pair. Position flags to mark a goal 4 yards wide at each end of the area. Players station in opposite goals, facing one another. Player 1 has the ball to begin play.

**Procedure:** Player 1 tosses the ball upward so it drops near the center of the area. Player 2 moves forward from his or her goal, jumps up, and attempts to score by heading the ball past player 1 through the goal. Players return to their respective goals after each header. Repeat 50 times. Players alternate turns heading to score.

**Scoring:** Award 1 point for each goal scored. The player who scores the most points wins.

**Practice tips:** Players should jump vertically upward, arch back at the waist, and snap their upper body forward to contact the ball on the flat surface of their forehead. They should keep their head firmly positioned with eyes open and mouth closed at moment of contact with the ball.

# 51 Heading Race

**Minutes:** 10

**Players:** 8 to 14 (2 equal-sized teams of 4 to 7)

**Objective:** To improve heading technique

**Setup:** Teams position side by side in single file. Maintain at least three yards between teams. One player for each team plays as the server, who positions two yards in front of the team, facing the first player in line. Each server has a ball.

**Procedure:** On your command, servers toss a ball to the first player in their line, who heads it back to the server and immediately drops to their knees. The server catches the ball and tosses it to the second player in line who also heads and then kneels. Servers continue through the team until all players have headed and are kneeling. The team whose players are all kneeling first wins the race. Players then stand and rotate positions in preparation for the next round. The original server moves to the back of the line, the first player in line becomes the server, and everyone else moves one spot forward.

**Scoring:** The first team to win six races wins the series.

**Practice tips:** Encourage your players to arch their upper trunk back with their neck stiff and chin tucked and then to snap forward to meet the ball as it arrives. Players should keep their eyes open and their mouths closed. Contact with the ball should be with the flat surface of the forehead, just above the eyebrows.

# 52 Diving Headers

**Minutes:** 10 to 15 (or to a set number of points)

**Players:** 9 to 13 (2 equal-sized teams of 3 to 5; 2 servers; 1 goalkeeper)

**Objective:** To score goals with diving headers

**Setup:** Play on one end of a regulation field with a full-size goal centered on the endline. Divide your group into two teams of equal numbers. Position teams side by side in single file, about 15 yards from the goal. Station a server 6 yards to each side of the goal, about 6 yards out from the endline. Each server has plenty of balls. The neutral goalkeeper positions within the goal.

**Procedure:** Servers alternate tossing balls into the area 8 to 10 yards front and center of the goal. Tosses should be parallel to the ground at a height of about 3 or 4 feet. Players alternate attempting to score off of diving headers. The goalkeeper attempts to save all shots. Continue the exercise until each player has attempted at least 10 diving headers.

**Scoring:** Award 2 points for a goal scored via a diving header and 1 point for a ball on goal saved by the goalkeeper. The team scoring the most points wins.

**Practice tips:** Dive headers are especially fun to practice on a wet, soggy field. However, correct technique is essential to prevent injury. Players should dive forward parallel to the ground with head tilted back and neck firm. The ball should be contacted on the flat surface of the forehead, with eyes open and mouth closed. Arms and hands should extend down to cushion the impact with the ground. This game is not recommended for young players (10 years and under) who lack adequate strength and coordination.

# 53 Headers Only

**Minutes:** 15

**Players:** 12 to 16 (2 teams of 4 to 6; 4 neutral players)

**Objective:** To score from headers and develop endurance

**Setup:** Use markers to form a rectangular area 40 by 50 yards. Put a small goal 4 yards wide at the midpoint of each endline. Designate four neutral players, who always join the team with possession of the ball. Use colored vests to differentiate teams. Award one team possession of the ball to begin. No goalkeepers are needed.

**Procedure:** Each team defends a goal. Pass the ball by throwing and catching rather than kicking. Players may take up to five steps with the ball before passing it to a teammate. Violation of the five-step rule results in losing possession to the opposing team. Neutral players join with the team in possession to create a four-player advantage for the attack. There are no goalkeepers, but all players may intercept passes or block shots with their hands. Points are scored by heading a ball tossed by a teammate through the opponent's goal.

Defending players gain possession of the ball when they intercept an opponent's pass, when an opponent drops the ball to the ground, when an opponent takes more than five steps with the ball, or when the ball is played out of bounds by an opponent. Defenders may not wrestle the ball from an opponent.

**Scoring:** The team scoring the most points wins.

**Practice tips:** Player movement should simulate the patterns (positioning) used in an actual soccer game. Support players should position at wide angles with clear passing lanes to the ball. Emphasize proper heading technique. Players should head the ball on a downward plane toward the goal line when attempting to score.

# 54 Off the Turn

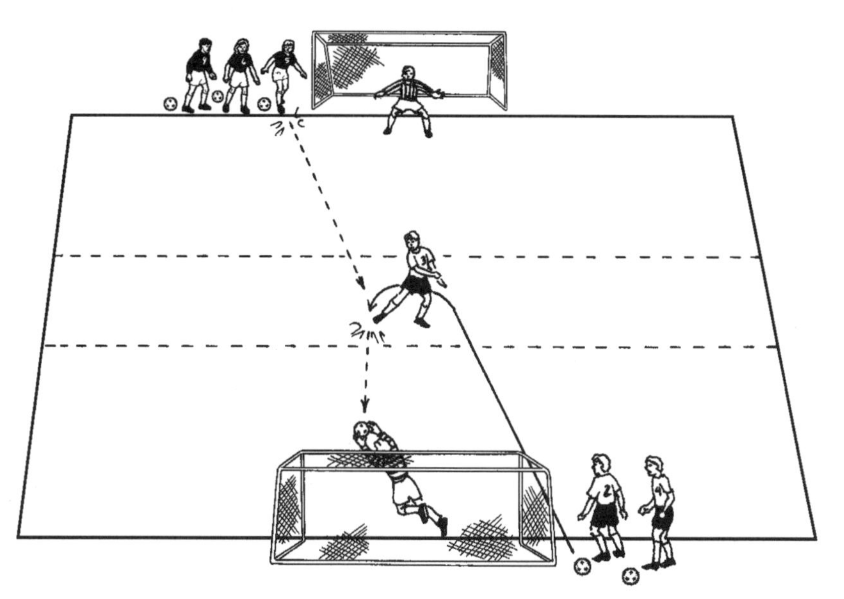

**Minutes:** 15

**Players:** 8 (2 groups of 3 shooters; 2 goalkeepers)

**Objective:** To receive, turn, and shoot at goal using only two touches

**Setup:** Play on one end of a regulation field. Position markers to extend the penalty area to 36 yards (twice its normal length). Position a full-size goal on each endline with a goalkeeper in each goal. Mark a neutral zone 5 yards deep at the center of the playing area. Divide players into two groups of three (groups A and B). Position groups on opposite endlines diagonally across (on opposite sides of the goal) from one another. Give each group several balls.

**Procedure:** To begin, player B (shooter) sprints forward off the endline and into the neutral zone. Player A (server) stationed on the opposite endline simultaneously passes a ball toward player B. Player B receives and turns the ball 180 degrees with the first touch, then shoots to score with the second touch. The shooter follows up the shot, in case of a rebound off the keeper, and then returns to his or her team, after which the next pair of players takes their turn. Teams alternate serving and shooting.

**Scoring:** Award 1 point for each goal scored. The player who scores the most points wins.

**Practice tips:** Players should check hard toward the server to receive the pass, just as they would in actual game situations. The ball should be received and turned in one fluid motion. As a variation, the server may play balls through the air as well as along the ground.

# 55 Dribble the Maze and Score

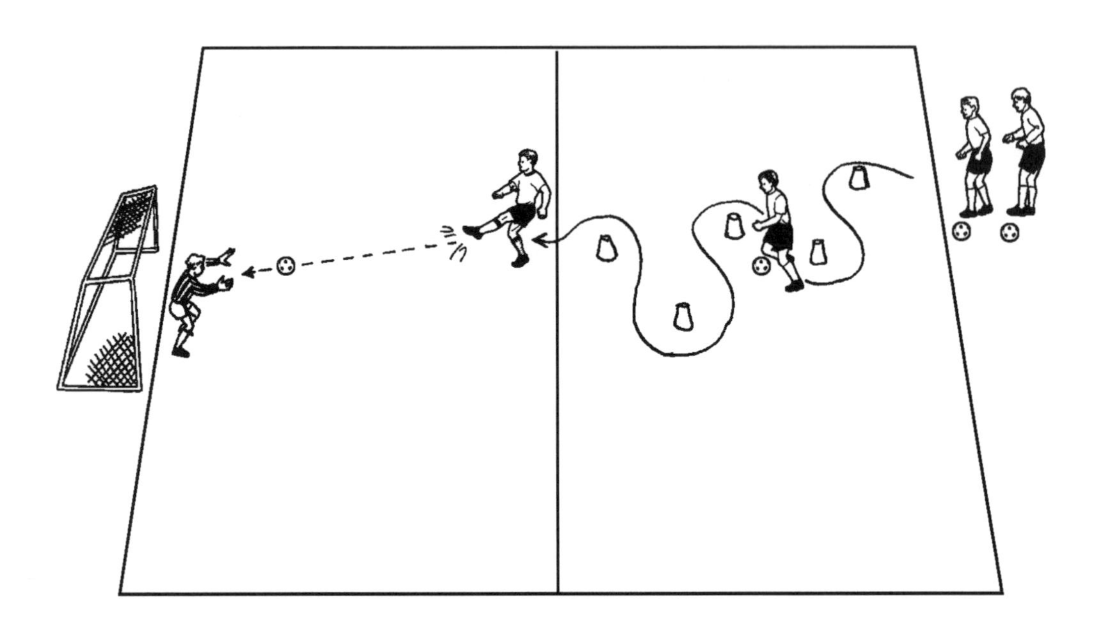

**Minutes:** 10 to 15

**Players:** 4 to 6 (3 to 5 shooters; 1 goalkeeper)

**Objectives:** To shoot with power and accuracy; to dribble with close control in tight spaces; to provide goalkeeper training

**Setup:** Use markers to form a rectangular area 30 by 40 yards, divided lengthwise by a midline. Position a regulation goal at the midpoint of one endline. Shooters, each with a ball, station at the opposite endline. Place cones or flags to represent five small goals, arranged in a zigzag pattern, in the half of the field occupied by the shooters. Put a goalkeeper in the regulation goal.

**Procedure:** Shooters, in turn, dribble at top speed through the five mini-goals. After going through the last goal, they push the ball into the goalkeeper's half of the field, sprint to it, and shoot to score. Shooters retrieve their ball and return to the starting position. Continue until each player has attempted 20 shots at goal.

**Scoring:** Award shooters 2 points for a goal scored and 1 point for a shot on goal saved by the goalkeeper. The player with the most points wins.

**Practice tips:** Position the mini-goals so that shooters are required to cut the ball sharply and change direction when dribbling through them. Emphasize dribbling speed and control.

# 56 Rapid Fire

**Minutes:** 15

**Players:** Groups of 3

**Objectives:** To develop shooting skills under simulated match pressures; to improve fitness

**Setup:** Play on one end of a regulation field with a full-size goal centered on the endline. Designate one player as shooter, one as server, and one as goalkeeper. The shooter positions 25 yards from the endline, with his or her back to the goal. The server stations 30 yards from the goal facing the shooter, with 8 to 10 balls. The goalkeeper positions within the goal.

**Procedure:** The server plays a ball past the shooter (toward the goal) who quickly turns, sprints to the ball, and shoots to score. The shooter must strike the ball first time (one touch), then immediately sprint back to the start position. The server immediately plays another ball past the shooter, this time to the opposite side. Continue shooting until the supply of balls is depleted. The goalkeeper tries to save all shots. The players rotate positions (server or shooter) after each round. Play several rounds.

**Scoring:** Shooters are awarded 1 point for a shot on goal and 2 points for a goal scored. The player who scores the most points wins the round.

**Practice tips:** Have shooters sprint to the ball, taking the most direct route. Require first-time shots. Alternate shots with right and left feet. Reduce the shooting distance for younger players.

# 57 Serve and Shoot

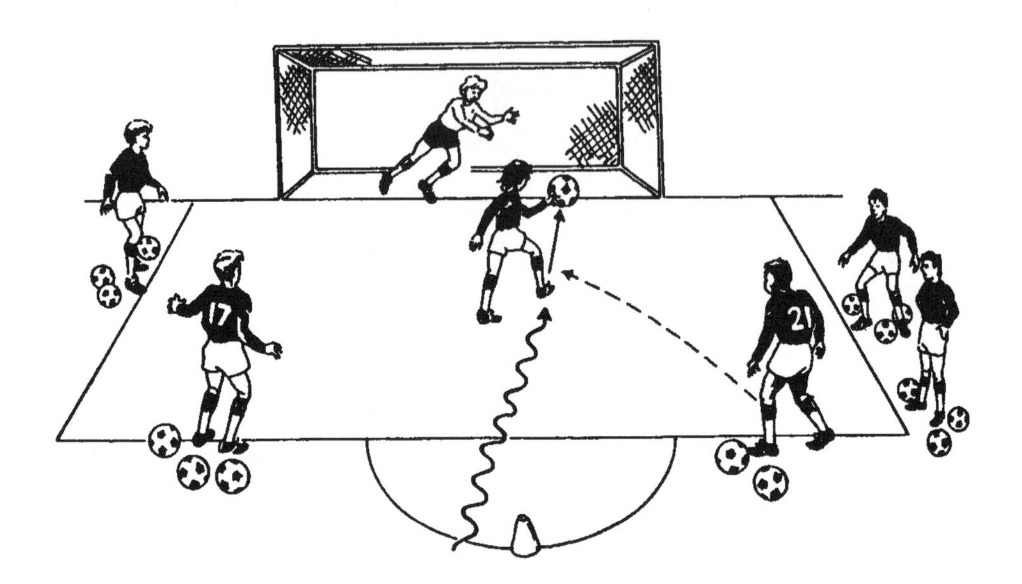


**Minutes:** 3 per round

**Players:** 7 (1 shooter; 5 servers; 1 goalkeeper)

**Objectives:** To shoot with power and accuracy; to improve fitness; to provide goalkeeper training

**Setup:** Play on one end of a regulation field with a full-size goal. Position a cone on the front edge of the penalty arc, about 22 yards from the goal. Position five servers, each with a supply of balls, around the perimeter of the penalty area. The shooter positions on the penalty arc next to the cone. The goalkeeper stations within the goal.

**Procedure:** Server 1 pushes a ball into the penalty area. The shooter moves quickly to the ball, controls it toward goal with the first touch, and shoots to score with the second touch. The shooter sprints back to the cone and then sprints to a ball pushed into the penalty area by server 2. The goalkeeper attempts to save all shots. Continue for 10 consecutive shots, after which the shooter switches positions with one of the servers, and the round is repeated with a different shooter. Continue until all players have taken two turns as the shooter.

**Scoring:** Award 1 point for a shot on goal and 2 points for a goal scored. The player who scores the most points wins.

**Practice tips:** Vary the type of service (rolling, bouncing, lofted balls). As a variation, require first-time (one-touch) shooting or add a pressuring defender.

# 58 Shoot to Score

**Minutes:** 15 to 20

**Players:** 6 (2 teams of 2; 1 server; 1 goalkeeper)

**Objectives:** To develop shooting skills under game-simulated pressures of limited space and physical fatigue; to improve fitness; to provide goalkeeper training

**Setup:** Play on one end of a regulation field with a full-size goal on the endline. Form two teams of two; station both teams within the penalty area. Position a server at the top (front edge) of the penalty area with a dozen balls. The goalkeeper stations within the common goal.

**Procedure:** To begin, the server plays a ball into the penalty area, where both teams vie for possession. The team gaining possession attempts to score, while their opponents defend. Teams immediately switch roles upon change of possession. The keeper attempts to save all shots. Play stops momentarily after a goal is scored, when the keeper makes a save, or when the ball is kicked out of bounds. The server immediately restarts play by kicking another ball into the area. Continue nonstop until the supply of balls is used up. Repeat the round after a short rest.

**Scoring:** The team scoring the most goals wins the round. Play five rounds.

**Practice tips:** Players must recognize scoring opportunities and release shots at any chance. Emphasize quick release and accuracy rather than pure power.

# 59 3 (+1) Versus 3 (+1) Shooting

**Minutes:** 15 to 20

**Players:** 10 (8 field players; 2 goalkeepers)

**Objectives:** To develop long-distance shooting skills; to develop combination play among attacking players

**Setup:** Use markers to extend the penalty area to twice its length, creating a field area 36 yards long and 44 yards wide. Position a full-size goal on each endline. You'll need one ball per game, plus an extra supply of balls in each goal.

**Procedure:** Form teams of four field players and one goalkeeper. Each team positions three players in its defending half and one player in the opponent's half of the field, creating a 3 v 1 situation in each zone. Players are restricted to movement within their assigned zone. Play begins with the goalkeeper distributing the ball to one of the three teammates stationed in the defending zone, who then attempt to score on the opposing keeper. The single opponent stationed in that zone attempts to prevent shots on his or her goalkeeper. Players are restricted to two touches or fewer to receive, pass, and shoot the ball. All shots must originate from the team's defending half of the field. The fourth member of the team, positioned in the opposite half, can follow up shots on goal to finish any rebounds that come off the opposing keeper. After each shot at goal or change of possession, the defending goalkeeper restarts play by distributing the ball to a teammate stationed in his or her team's defending zone.

**Scoring:** Award 1 point for each shot on goal, 2 points for a goal scored. Team scoring the most points wins.

**Practice tips:** The 3 v 1 player advantage in each zone should promote numerous long-range scoring opportunities. Encourage quick ball movement to create open shooting lanes to goal. Emphasize proper instep shooting technique.

# 60 One Central Goal

**Minutes:** 15 to 20

**Players:** 7 to 11 (2 equal-sized teams of 3 to 5; 1 neutral goalkeeper)

**Objectives:** To develop shooting skills; to provide shot-stopping practice for goalkeeper; to improve endurance

**Setup:** Use markers to outline an area about 40 yards square. Position two flags in the center of the area to represent a full-size goal. The neutral goalkeeper stations within the goal. Award one team possession of the ball. Use colored vests to differentiate teams.

**Procedure:** Begin with a kickoff with the ball spotted along a perimeter line of the area. Teams can score through either side of the central goal, so the goalkeeper must constantly readjust position in response to movement of the ball. After each save, the goalkeeper tosses the ball toward a corner of the playing area, where teams vie for possession. Change of possession occurs after a scored goal, when the ball travels out of the field area, or when a defending player steals the ball. A ball played out-of-bounds is returned by a throw-in. Regular soccer rules are in effect except that the offside rule is waived.

**Scoring:** A shot traveling through the goal below the height of the goalkeeper's head counts as a goal scored. The team scoring the most goals wins.

**Practice tips:** Place restrictions on players (such as only two-touch or three-touch passes).

# 61 World Cup Scoring

**Minutes:** 20 to 30

**Players:** 9 to 13 (8 to 12 field players, in pairs; 1 goalkeeper)

**Objective:** To release shots under the game-simulated pressures of limited time, restricted space, and challenging opponents

**Setup:** Play within the penalty area of a regulation field with a full-size goal centered on the endline. Place a supply of balls inside the goal. Organize teams of two players each. Each team chooses a country to represent (USA, England, Germany, etc.). All teams station within the penalty area. The neutral goalkeeper positions within the goal.

**Procedure:** The game begins with the goalkeeper tossing a couple of balls toward the outer edge of the penalty area. Teams vie for possession. Teams gaining possession of a ball attempt to score in the full-size goal, while other teams defend. The offside rule is not in effect. A team that loses possession immediately defends, whereas a team gaining possession immediately attacks. After each save, the goalkeeper returns the ball into play by tossing it toward the edge of the penalty area. Two balls are kept in play at all times. A team that scores on the keeper advances to the next round of play. Players must shout their country name and sprint off the field (behind the goal) after scoring to wait for the next round to begin. The round ends when all teams but one have scored. That team is eliminated from the competition. Teams that score advance to the next round, which is played in the same manner as the first. Complete a sufficient number of rounds until only one team remains—the World Cup champion.

**Scoring:** Normal soccer rules apply except that the offside rule is waived.

**Practice tips:** The focus is on scoring goals under game-simulated conditions. Encourage players to shoot at every opportunity. No slide tackles.

# 62 Scoring Long Distance

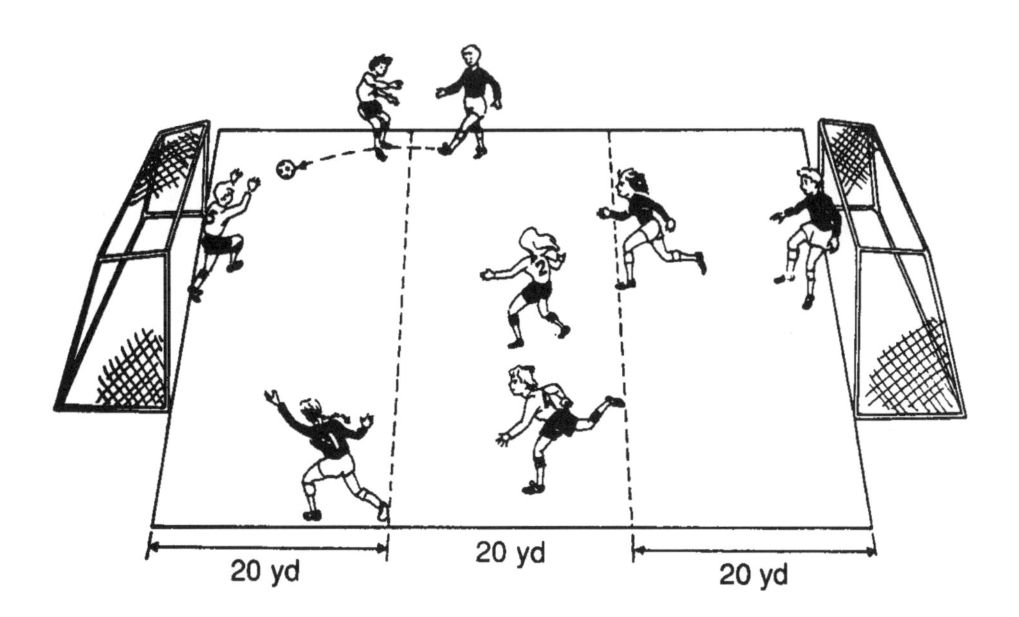


**Minutes:** 15 to 20

**Players:** 8 (2 teams of 3 field players; 2 goalkeepers)

**Objectives:** To shoot with power and accuracy from outside the penalty area; to improve general endurance; to provide goalkeeper training

**Setup:** Use markers to form a rectangular area 40 by 60 yards. Position a regulation goal at the midpoint of each endline. Use markers to further divide the field into three equal 20- by 40-yard zones. Organize two teams of three field players and one goalkeeper. Each team defends a goal. Award one team the ball to begin.

**Procedure:** Begin with a kickoff from the center of the field. Regular soccer rules apply, except that all shots must originate from within the middle zone, 20 yards or more from the goal. Players are permitted to score from within the end zones but only off a rebound off the goalkeeper.

**Scoring:** Award 3 points for a goal scored and 1 point for a shot on goal saved by the goalkeeper. The team scoring the most points wins.

**Practice tips:** Adjust the area size to the age and abilities of your players. For example, require players 12 years old and under to take shots from a distance of 15 yards or greater.

# 63 Volley Shooting

**Minutes:** 20 to 25

**Players:** 8 to 12 (2 equal-sized teams of 4 to 6)

**Objectives:** To score off of volley shots; to develop general endurance

**Setup:** Use markers to form a rectangular playing area 40 by 60 yards. Position a full-size goal on the center of each endline. Form two teams of equal numbers. Award one team the ball to begin. Use colored vests to differentiate teams. No goalkeepers are needed.

**Procedure:** Each team defends a goal. Players pass the ball by throwing (and catching) rather than kicking. A player may take no more than five steps with the ball before releasing it to a teammate. Change of possession occurs when a defending player intercepts a pass, the ball goes out of play last touched by an attacking player, the ball is dropped to the ground, a player takes more than five steps with the ball, or a goal is scored. Points are scored by volleying the ball through the opponent's goal. Players must volley a ball tossed by a teammate; they can't toss the ball to themselves. Although goalkeepers are not used, all players are permitted to use their hands to catch the ball and block passes or shots.

**Scoring:** The team scoring the most goals wins.

**Practice tips:** To execute full-volley shots requires precise timing and correct technique, so this game might not be appropriate for young or inexperienced players. Teammates should move up and down the field as a compact unit, supporting one another and making themselves available for passes.

# Part V

# Tactical Training Games

Soccer tactics involve decision-making, problem-solving, and playing in combination with teammates to achieve a common goal. To make the most appropriate choices in the heat of game competition requires a thorough understanding of the tactical concepts on which player actions are based. Decisions such as when to release the ball, where to position in relation to the ball and opponents, how to defend when outnumbered, and whether to shoot, dribble, or pass in a specific situation are just a few examples of the many choices that confront players during a match. Being able to make correct split-second judgments under the pressures of match competition is just as important as being able to successfully perform the skills required in those situations. Players who make the right decisions most often experience the greatest success.

Tactics are applied at three levels—individual, group, and team. Individual tactics encompass the principles of attack and defense that apply in one-on-one situations. Group tactics involve three or more players in combination. Tactics are also applied to the team as a whole, particularly regarding player roles and systems of play. The ultimate objective of team tactics (7 v 5, 9 v 6, etc.) is to make the whole team greater than the sum of its individual parts.

Tactical training begins with the most fundamental tactical unit (1 v 1), progresses to small group (2 v 1, 2 v 2, and 3 v 2) situations, and gradually evolves into large group, or team, tactics. It's important to consider that tactics are of little or no use if players cannot execute basic soccer skills. For this reason, the teaching of tactics should not be emphasized until players are competent in performing the basic soccer skills. Simply put, younger players should focus on skill development rather than tactical training.

The games in this section are mainly arranged in a progressive sequence, beginning with individual tactics and progressing through group situations. All games can and should be adapted to the age, abilities, and developmental level of your players. By altering factors such as size of the playing area, number of players, types of passes required, number of touches allowed to pass and receive the ball, and the speed of repetition, you can make the games either more or less challenging for your players.

# 64 1 v 1 to Common Goal

**Minutes:** 60 seconds per game (minimum of 5 games)

**Players:** Unlimited (in pairs)

**Objectives:** To develop the individual attacking and defending tactics used in a one-on-one situation; to improve dribbling, tackling, and shielding skills; to improve fitness

**Setup:** Use markers to create a 15-yard square playing area for each pair of players. Position flags to represent a common goal two yards wide in the center of the area. You'll need one ball per pair.

**Procedure:** Partners play 1 v 1 within the area. Players score by passing or dribbling the ball through the goal. Points can be scored through either side of the common goal. Change of possession occurs when the defending player steals the ball, after a goal is scored, or when the ball travels out of the area. Players reverse roles immediately with each change of possession. Play a series of 1-minute games with 30 seconds rest between games.

**Scoring:** Player scoring the most points wins.

**Practice tips:** Increase the size of the goal and shorten the game to 30 seconds for young (10 years old and under) players.

# 65 Attack and Defend (1 v 1)

**Minutes:** 15

**Players:** Unlimited (in pairs)

**Objective:** To attack and defend in a one-on-one situation

**Setup:** Players (A and B) pair up for competition. Use markers to create a 15-yard by 25-yard field for each pair. Position flags to represent a goal four yards wide on each endline. Partners position in opposite goals facing one another. Player A has the ball to begin.

**Procedure:** Player A serves a lofted pass to Player B and then moves forward to play as a defender. Player B receives the ball and attempts to take on and beat A by dribbling past him or her through the goal. After a score or change of possession, both players return to their respective goals and repeat the round. Players alternate playing as the defender and attacker.

**Scoring:** Award 1 point for each score. The player scoring the most points wins.

**Practice tips:** Encourage the attacker to take on the defender at speed. The defender tries to deny penetration via the dribble. He or she should quickly close the distance to the attacker and assume the proper defensive posture. Reduce the area size for younger players.

# 66 1 v 1 With Support

**Minutes:** 2-minute rounds

**Players:** 4 (2 teams of 2)

**Objectives:** To develop individual attack and defense tactics; to improve dribbling and tackling skills; to develop fitness

**Setup:** Form two teams of two. Use markers to create a 10-yard by 20-yard playing area for each game. One player on each team functions as a "goal" by standing on his or her respective endline with feet spread wide apart. Goals must remain stationary throughout the two-minute game. Remaining players station in the center of the area. One (attacker) has the ball to begin; the other defends.

**Procedure:** Central players compete 1 v 1. Points are scored by kicking the ball through the opponent's goal (legs). If the defending player steals the ball, he or she immediately becomes the attacker, and vice versa. Players positioned as goals may not stop an opponent's shot from rolling through their legs. Central players are permitted to play the ball back to their own goal, however, and can receive a return pass from the goal player, but the goal player is not permitted to move forward off of the endline in support of his or her teammate. Change of possession occurs when the defender steals the ball, when the ball travels out of play, and after each score. Play two-minute rounds. Teammates switch positions after each round; the "goal" becomes the field player and vice versa.

**Scoring:** The player scoring the most goals wins the round. The first team to win five rounds wins the game.

**Practice tips:** Players playing as goals have extra soccer balls nearby. When the game ball is kicked out of the area, the goal player can immediately put another ball into play to keep action continuous. As a variation, add sideline support players.

# 67 Multiple 1 v 1 Possession

**Minutes:** 20, divided into 2-minute rounds

**Players:** 8 (3 teams of 2; 2 neutral players)

**Objectives:** To practice individual attack and defense tactics; to develop dribbling and shielding skills; to improve tackling skills

**Setup:** Use markers to create a 25-yard by 30-yard playing area. Form three player pairs. Designate two additional players as neutrals, who wear a distinctive colored jersey. One member of each team has a ball to begin. Neutral players do not have a ball.

**Procedure:** Player with the ball (attacker) tries to keep possession by dribbling away from or shielding the ball from his or her partner (defender), who attempts to gain possession. The attacker is allowed to combine (pass to) with the neutral players, when possible, to maintain possession. Neutral players are restricted to three or fewer touches to receive and return the ball to the attacker. If the defender steals the ball, players immediately reverse roles—the original attacker becomes the defender and vice versa. Play for two minutes. Repeat after a short rest. Play a total of 8 to 10 games.

**Scoring:** None

**Practice tips:** Attackers should look to execute a give-and-go pass with a neutral player when the opportunity is available. Adjust the area size to accommodate the age and ability of your players. As a variation, add additional neutral players to the exercise.

# 68 Attack 1 v 2

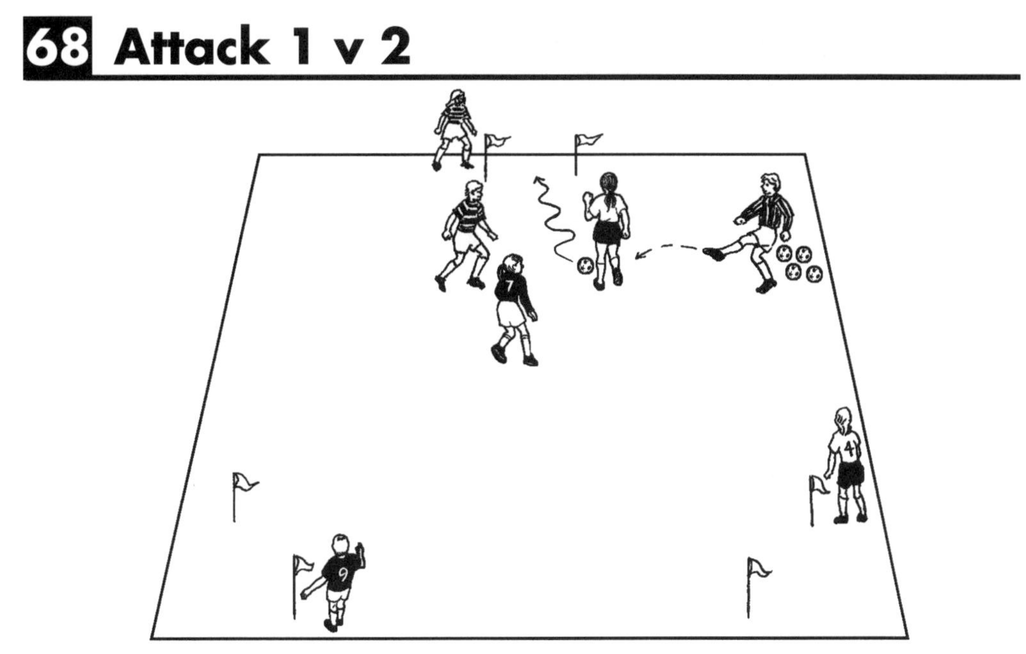

**Minutes:** 15 to 20

**Players:** 7 (3 teams of 2; 1 server)

**Objectives:** To take on and beat an opponent (and in some cases two opponents) in tight spaces; to possess the ball under intense defensive pressure; to develop endurance

**Setup:** Use flags to form three small goals. Position goals in the form of a triangle, with at least 15 yards between them. Form three teams of two. One member of each pair stations outside the triangle, near a goal. One member of each pair stations within the triangular field area formed by the goals. Position a server to the side of the field with an ample supply of soccer balls.

**Procedure:** The exercise begins as the server kicks a ball into the triangle. The player who receives the ball (attacker) competes 1 v 2 against the other middle players (defenders). The attacker can score points by dribbling the ball through any of the three goals. Points may be scored through either side of a goal, but the attacker is not permitted to dribble through the same goal twice in succession. If a defender steals the ball, he or she immediately becomes the attacker, while the original attacker becomes a defender.

Players stationed outside the triangle (next to the goals) are passive until their partner tags them. When a player is tagged, he or she enters the triangle and assumes the role of his or her partner; the partner then stations outside of the triangle to rest. Play is continuous.

**Scoring:** Award 1 point each time a player dribbles through a goal. Keep track of total points scored by each team.

**Practice tips:** Dribbling is an effective means of penetrating a packed defense. Encourage sudden changes of speed and direction coupled with deceptive body feints to beat defenders. No slide tackles.

# 69 1 v 2 in the Box

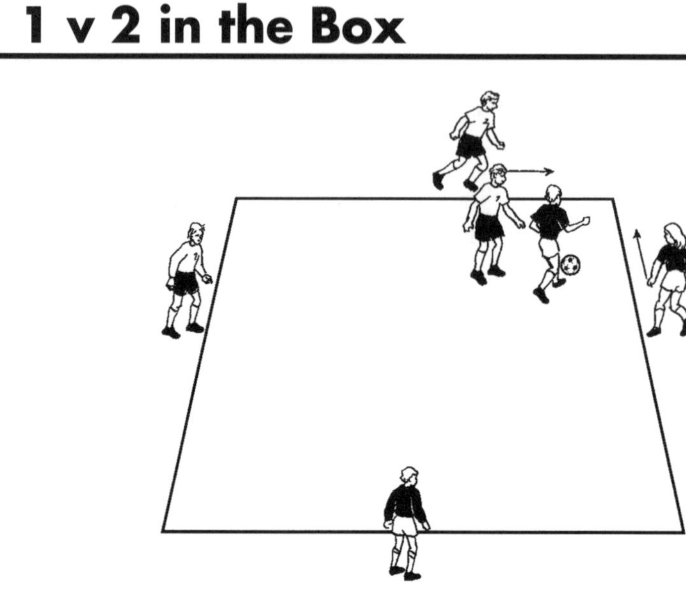

**Minutes:** 12 to 15

**Players:** 6 (3 teams of 2)

**Objectives:** To penetrate a layered defense; to improve dribbling and shielding skills

**Setup:** Use markers to create a field area 20 yards square. Form three groups of two. One pair stations within the field, where partners compete 1 v 1. Remaining players play as neutral defenders and position on the perimeter of the area, one on each sideline. Sideline defenders are responsible for preventing the player with the ball from dribbling out of the square and can move laterally along their sideline to intercept a dribbler. Defenders can move two yards inward off the sideline to challenge an attacker who is dribbling at them, but they may not chase the attacker into the center of the square.

**Procedure:** Player with the ball (attacker) scores 1 point by dribbling out of the box; the opponent (defender) tries to prevent scores. Partners reverse roles immediately upon change of possession. Neutral defenders stationed along the sidelines assist the central defender in preventing the attacker from dribbling out of the field area, creating a 1 v 2 advantage for the defense when the attacker nears a sideline. Play a series of three-minute games, with a different pair competing in each game.

**Scoring:** Award 1 point to a player who dribbles the ball over a sideline. After each score, partners exchange possession of the ball and return within the field area, where play resumes. The player scoring the most points in three minutes wins.

**Practice tips:** Encourage defenders to double down on the attacker as he or she nears the sideline. Adjust the size of the playing area to accommodate the age and ability of your players. As a variation, place two neutral defenders on each sideline.

# 70 Play the Wall (2 v 1)

**Minutes:** 15

**Players:** 3

**Objectives:** To use the wall (give-and-go) pass to beat a defender; to defend in an outnumbered situation

**Setup:** Use markers to create a 12-yard square area for each group. Designate two players as attackers and one as defender. You'll need one ball per group.

**Procedure:** Attackers attempt to keep the ball from the defender by dribbling and passing to each other. Emphasize using the give-and-go (wall) pass to beat the defender. To perform a wall pass, the player on the ball passes to his or her teammate and immediately sprints behind the defender to collect a one-touch return pass. If the defender steals the ball, he or she immediately returns it to the attackers, and the game continues. Play three five-minute games, with each player taking a turn as the defender.

**Scoring:** Attackers earn 1 point for five passes without a possession loss and 2 points for each time they successfully execute a wall pass. Defender scores 2 points each time he or she wins possession of the ball or forces the attackers to play the ball outside the area. Player (attacker or defender) scoring the most points in five minutes wins the game.

**Practice tips:** Execution of the wall pass requires skill, timing, anticipation, and teamwork. The player with the ball must commit (dribble at) the defender toward him or her. At the same time, the supporting teammate must position nearby with an open passing lane to the ball. Increase the area size for beginning players to allow attackers more time to execute skills and make decisions.

# 71 2 v 1 to Endline

**Minutes:** 15

**Players:** 3

**Objectives:** To attack and defend in a 2 v 1 situation; to develop dribbling, passing, and tackling skills

**Setup:** Use markers to create a 10-yard by 30-yard area. Station one player (defender) on an endline with a ball. Station two players (attackers) on the opposite endline.

**Procedure:** Defender initiates play by serving the ball to the attackers, then moves forward off the endline. Attackers control the ball and advance to take on the defender 2 v 1. The objective is to bypass the defender, either via the dribble or by executing a give-and-go pass, and dribble the ball over the endline. Attackers must stay within the 10-yard wide channel when attempting to beat the defender. The round ends when the defender steals the ball or the attackers advance the ball under control over the endline, whichever occurs first. Players immediately return to their original positions and repeat the round.

**Scoring:** The defender gets 1 point for dispossessing the attackers or for forcing them to play the ball out of the area. Attackers get 1 point when they beat the defender and dribble the ball across the endline. Play to 10 points, then rotate positions and repeat. Play three rounds, with each player taking a turn as the defender.

**Practice tips:** Attackers should dribble at (commit) the defender at speed. Encourage players to look for opportunities to execute the wall pass.

# 72 2 v 1 (+1) Transition

**Minutes:** 15 to 20

**Players:** 4 (2 teams of 2)

**Objectives:** To use the wall pass to beat an opponent; to defend when outnumbered; to develop immediate transition from attack to defense and vice versa

**Setup:** Use markers to create a 15-yard by 25-yard area for each game. Position flags to represent a goal 4 yards wide at the midpoint of each endline. Form two-player teams. One team has the ball to begin. No goalkeepers required.

**Procedure:** Begin with a kickoff from the center of the field. Each team defends a goal and can score in the opponent's goal. The team with the ball attacks with two players; the defending team positions one player as the goalkeeper and the other as a single defender. Change of possession occurs when the defender steals the ball, the goalkeeper makes a save, the ball goes out of the field area last touched by an attacker, or after a score. A defender who steals the ball must pass it back to the goalkeeper before the team can counterattack. After receiving the ball, either from his or her teammate or by making a save, the goalkeeper immediately moves forward to join his or her teammate to attack the opponent's goal. One player on the opposing team immediately sprints back to the goal to play goalkeeper, while his or her teammate plays as the single defender. Teammates alternate turns playing as the goalkeeper.

**Scoring:** Award 1 point for each goal. The team scoring the most points wins.

**Practice tips:** Emphasize quick transitional play. When possible, attackers should commit the defender to the ball and then execute the wall (give-and-go) pass.

# 73 Wide-Angle Support (3 v 1)

**Minutes:** 20 (5-minute rounds)

**Players:** 4

**Objectives:** To position at the proper angle and depth of support; to pass and receive the ball effectively under game-simulated pressures; to defend when outnumbered

**Setup:** Use markers to create a 12-yard square area for each group. Designate 3 attackers and 1 defender. You'll need one ball per group.

**Procedure:** Attackers try to keep the ball from the defender by passing among themselves. If the defender steals the ball or kicks it out of the area, the ball is immediately returned to an attacker, and the game continues. Play five minutes, then designate a different player as the defender. Play four rounds so all players have a turn at defending.

**Scoring:** The attacking team scores 1 point for eight consecutive passes without possession loss. The defender gets 1 point each time he or she steals the ball or causes the attackers to play the ball out of the area. The team scoring the most points after five minutes wins.

**Practice tips:** Encourage players to position at the correct angle and depth of support to provide clear passing lanes for the teammate with the ball. Impose restrictions to make the game more challenging (such as limiting attackers to three touches or fewer to pass and receive the ball). For beginners, increase the playing area size and reduce the number of consecutive passes required to score.

# 74 Last Player In

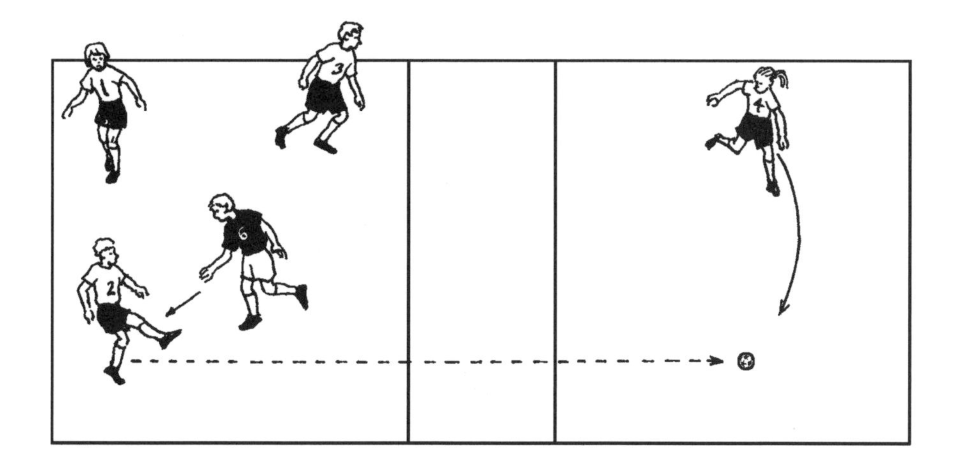

**Minutes:** 15

**Players:** 5

**Objectives:** To develop proper angles of support among attacking players; to develop passing skills and decision-making ability under game-simulated pressures

**Setup:** Use markers to create two 12-yard by 12-yard grids about 10 yards apart. Place three or four balls outside of each grid. Designate four players as attackers and one as a defender. Station three attackers and the defender in grid 1. The remaining attacker (target) positions in grid 2.

**Procedure:** The three attackers in grid 1 attempt to keep the ball from the defender. Attackers must complete at least four passes within the grid before passing the ball to the "target" in grid 2. The three attackers immediately sprint into grid 2 to support the ball. The last player to arrive becomes the defender in grid 2; the other two attackers plus the target combine to play 3 v 1 against the defender. The original defender remains in grid 1 as the target player for the next round.

The exercise continues as players move back and forth from one grid to the other. If the defender steals the ball, or kicks it out of the grid, he or she is replaced immediately by the attacker who lost possession of the ball, and the game continues. If the pass to the target in the opposite grid is not accurate (within the grid), play resumes, with the player who made the errant pass becoming the defender.

**Scoring:** Passes completed to target in the opposite grid score 1 point.

**Practice tips:** Emphasize proper support for player on the ball, both within the grid and once the ball has been played into the opposite grid. Attackers position at wide angles of support (greater than 45 degrees) to prevent the outnumbered defender from cutting off the passing lane.

# 75 2 v 2 Possession (With Support)

**Minutes:** 20 (5-minute rounds)

**Players:** 8 (2 teams of 2; 4 support players)

**Objective:** To develop passing combinations and support movement required to keep the ball from opponents

**Setup:** Use markers to create a 25-yard-square playing area. Place a cone at the midpoint of each sideline. Station a support player at each cone. Remaining players partner with a teammate to create two teams of two. Both teams position within the area; one team has the ball to begin. Use colored vests to differentiate teams.

**Procedure:** The team in possession tries to keep the ball from its opponents. Support players join with the team in possession to create a 6 v 2 player advantage for the attack. Support players are restricted in their movements. They can move laterally along their sideline but can't move inward off of the line. Support players are also limited to three or fewer touches to receive and pass the ball. Support players may receive the ball from, and pass it to, the central players only—they may not pass among themselves. Loss of possession occurs when a defending player steals the ball or the ball goes out of play. Play for five minutes, after which central players switch roles with support players. Play four games.

**Scoring:** Award 1 team point for eight passes without a possession loss. The team scoring the most points wins.

**Practice tips:** Impose restrictions to make the game more challenging for advanced players (such as limiting support players to one touch to return the ball or prohibiting them from passing the ball back to the same player who passed it to them). For young players, reduce the area size and award 1 point for five consecutive passes.

# 76 2 v 2 With Targets

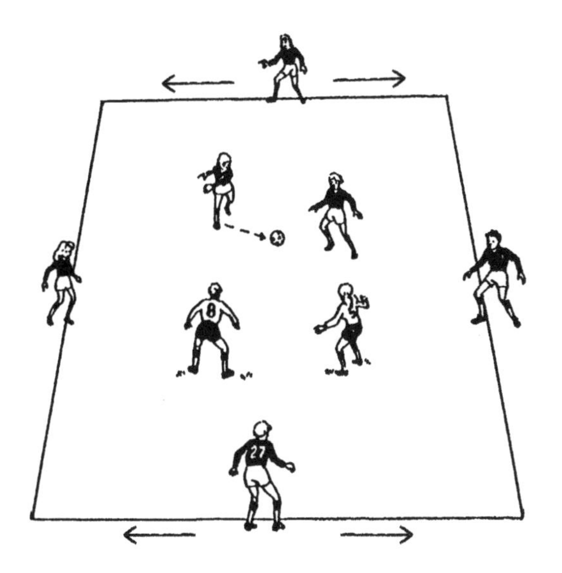

**Minutes:** 20

**Players:** 8 (2 teams of 2; 2 support players; 2 target players)

**Objectives:** To develop the team play required to penetrate opposing defenses; to practice the defensive concepts of pressure and cover

**Setup:** Use markers to create a 25-yard by 35-yard field. Form two teams of two players each, who station within the area. Put an additional player (target) at the midpoint of each endline and a support player at each sideline.

**Procedure:** Teams play 2 v 2 within the area, each team defending an endline. Goals are scored by passing the ball to the opponent's target, stationed on the endline. Central players are allowed to pass the ball to the sideline support players to create a 4 v 2 advantage for the attack. Support players are limited to two touches to pass and receive the ball. They can move along the side boundaries to receive passes but may not enter the field. However, support players may score points by passing to the defending team's target.

Defending players try to prevent opponents from completing a pass to the target stationed on their endline. Change of possession occurs after a goal is scored, when the ball goes out of bounds off an attacking player, or when a defending player steals the ball. Play for five minutes, after which support players and target players switch positions with central players, form teams of two players each, and repeat the game. Play four five-minute games.

**Scoring:** Attacking team scores 1 point for a pass completed to the target player stationed on the endline behind the defending team. The team scoring the most points in five minutes wins.

**Practice tips:** To make the game more challenging, place restrictions on advanced players (such as limiting support players to one- or two-touch passes).

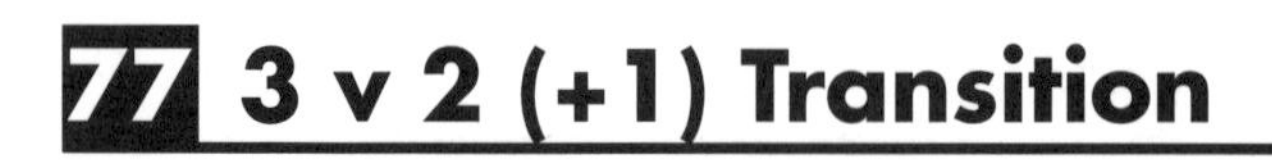

# 77 3 v 2 (+1) Transition

**Minutes:** 15 to 20

**Players:** 6 (2 teams of 3)

**Objectives:** To develop group tactics used in attack and defense; to coordinate movement of the first (pressuring) and second (covering) defenders; to improve transition play

**Setup:** Use markers to create a 20-yard by 30-yard playing area. Place two flags five yards apart at the midpoint of each endline to represent goals. Organize two three-player teams. Use colored vests to differentiate teams. One team has the ball to begin.

**Procedure:** Begin play with a kickoff from the center of the field. Each team defends a goal. The team with possession attacks with three players; opponents defend with two field players and a goalkeeper. A defending player who steals the ball must pass it back to his or her goalkeeper before initiating an attack on the opponent's goal. After receiving the ball, the goalkeeper moves forward to join his or her teammates to form a three-player attack. One player on the opposing team immediately retreats into the goal to play goalkeeper; the remaining two players position to defend the goal. Teams alternate between attack and defense on each change of possession. Teammates alternate playing goalkeeper.

**Scoring:** Goals are scored by kicking the ball through the opponent's goal below the height of the goalkeeper's head. The team scoring the most goals wins.

**Practice tips:** Emphasize immediate transition from defense to attack and vice versa on change of possession. Place extra balls behind each goal to avoid delays when a ball is shot past the goal. Adjust the area size to match the age and abilities of your players.

# 78 Skin the Defense (4 v 2)

**Minutes:** 24

**Players:** 6 (4 attackers; 2 defenders)

**Objectives:** To develop the combination play and player movement required to penetrate (split) the defense; to coordinate movement of the first (pressuring) and second (covering) defenders

**Setup:** Use markers to create a 12-yard by 24-yard area for each group. Designate four players as attackers and two as defenders. Use colored vests to differentiate teams. All players station within the area. One attacker has the ball.

**Procedure:** Attackers attempt to keep the ball from the defenders. When possible, they should split (pass the ball between) the two defenders. This type of pass is commonly referred to as the "killer" pass, as it penetrates the defense and puts defenders at a great disadvantage. If a defender steals the ball, or if the ball leaves the playing area, the ball is immediately returned to an attacker, and the game continues. Play for eight minutes, then designate two different players as defenders for the next round. Play three rounds, with all players taking a turn as defenders.

**Scoring:** The attacking team scores 1 point for eight consecutive passes without a loss of possession and 2 points for a pass that splits the defenders. Defenders get 1 point each time they gain possession of the ball or force attackers to play the ball out of the area. The team scoring the most points wins.

**Practice tips:** Attacking players should adjust their positions as the ball changes location. Support players should position at wide angles to either side of the ball to create open passing lanes. The defender nearest the ball (first defender) should apply pressure to the player on the ball to limit the time and space available to the attacker. The defender farthest from the ball (second defender) positions to prevent the killer pass. For highly skilled players, reduce the area size and limit the number of touches allowed to pass and receive the ball.

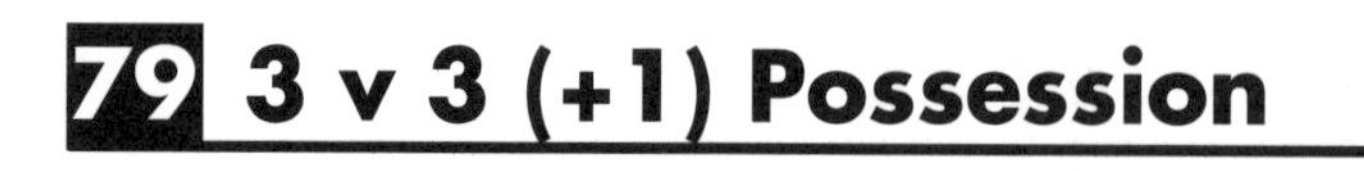

# 79 3 v 3 (+1) Possession

**Minutes:** 15 to 20

**Players:** 7 (2 teams of 3; 1 neutral player)

**Objectives:** To develop group attack and defense tactics; to improve passing, receiving, and dribbling skills under game-simulated conditions

**Setup:** Use markers to create a 30-yard by 30-yard playing area. Form two teams of three players each. Designate one additional player as a neutral player. Use colored vests to differentiate teams and the neutral player. You'll need one ball per game. Give one team possession of the ball.

**Procedure:** The team with the ball tries to keep it away from their opponents. The neutral player joins with the team in possession to create a 4 v 3 player advantage. Change of possession occurs when a defending player steals the ball or when the ball goes out of play last touched by a member of the attacking team. Play is continuous; teams switch from attack to defense and vice versa.

**Scoring:** Award 1 point for six consecutive passes without a loss of possession. The team scoring the most points wins.

**Practice tips:** Encourage quick ball movement along with proper depth and angle of support. On defense, emphasize the concepts of pressure, cover, and balance. Reduce the time and space available to advanced players by decreasing the area size.

# 80 Hot Potato (5 v 2)

**Minutes:** 15

**Players:** 7 (5 attackers; 2 defenders)

**Objectives:** To keep the ball from opponents through combination passing and proper support movement; to execute the defensive principles of pressure and cover; to develop passing and receiving skills

**Setup:** Use markers to create a 15-yard by 20-yard area for each group. Designate five attackers and two defenders. All players station within the area. Use colored vests to differentiate teams. You'll need one ball per group.

**Procedure:** Using two or fewer touches to receive and pass the ball, attackers try to keep the ball away from the outnumbered defenders. Attackers keep count of their consecutive passes. If a defender steals the ball, the ball goes out of play, or an attacker uses more than two touches to control and play the ball, the attackers must start the count over again. The defender who steals the ball immediately returns it to an attacker so that play continues uninterrupted.

**Scoring:** The attacking team earns 2 points for eight consecutive passes without a possession loss. Defenders get 1 point each time they intercept a pass or force attackers to lose control of the ball outside the playing area. Play until either defenders or attackers total 10 points, then repeat with different players as defenders.

**Practice tips:** The game is called "Hot Potato" because the ball moves constantly from one attacker to another. No one wants to be caught with the ball. Adjust the area size and touch restriction to match the age and abilities of your players. For example, to make the game more challenging, reduce the area size or require attacking players to play one touch.

# 81 Possess to Penetrate

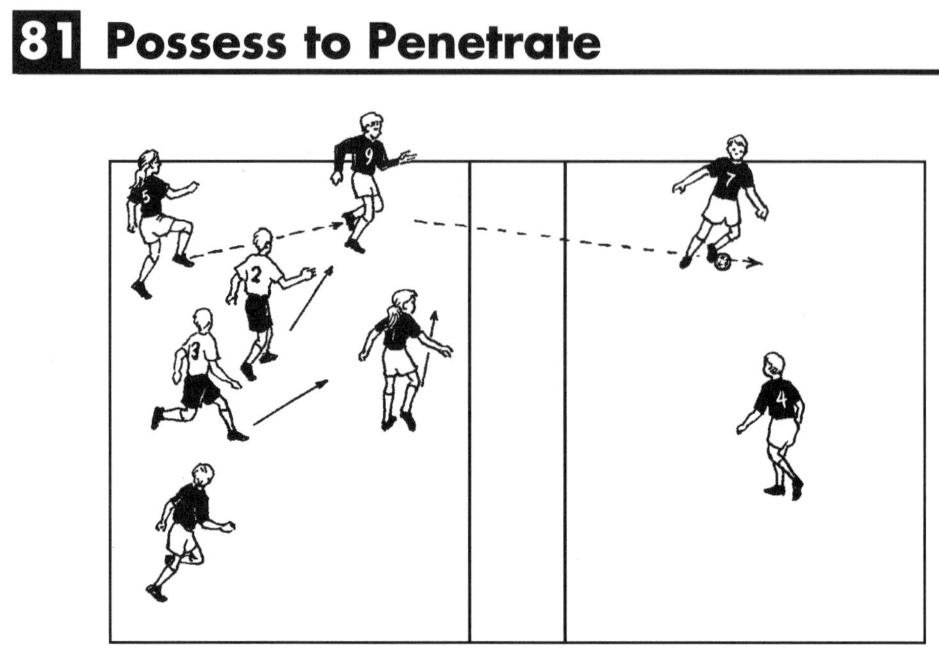

**Minutes:** 15-20

**Players:** 8 (6 attackers; 2 defenders)

**Objectives:** To develop group attack tactics; to possess the ball for the purpose of penetrating the defense; to defend when outnumbered

**Setup:** Use markers to create a 20-yard by 35-yard area divided into two grids (1 and 2), each 15 yards by 20 yards with a 5-yard deep neutral zone between them. Place four attackers and two defenders in grid 1 and two attackers in grid 2. Use colored vests to differentiate teams. Attackers in grid 1 have possession of the ball to begin. No goalkeepers.

**Procedure:** Four attackers in grid 1 play keep away from the two defenders. Attackers are limited to three or fewer touches to pass and receive the ball. After completing five or more consecutive passes, the attackers in grid 1 can play the ball to the attackers stationed in Grid 2. Two of the four attackers in grid 1 follow the ball into grid 2 to join the two attackers already stationed there. The two defenders in grid 1 quickly move into grid 2 to challenge for the ball, creating a 4 v 2 situation in grid 2. If defenders steal the ball or the ball travels outside of the grid, attackers immediately put another ball into play, and the game resumes. Play five minutes, with players switching from one grid to the other, then designate two different defenders and repeat the activity. Play several rounds.

**Scoring:** None

**Practice tips:** Emphasize quick ball movement, decision-making speed, and proper angles of support. The emphasis is on possession with the ultimate goal of penetration (passing to the adjacent grid), not merely possession for possession's sake.

# 82 4 v 2 (+2) With Four Goals

**Minutes:** 15 to 20

**Players:** 8 (2 teams of 4)

**Objective:** To develop group tactics used when attacking numbers-up (more players)

**Setup:** Use markers to create a 25-yard by 40-yard playing area. Position flags to form two goals 5 yards wide on each endline and spaced about 10 yards apart. Organize two teams of four players. Use colored vests to differentiate teams. Award one team possession of the ball to begin.

**Procedure:** The game begins with a kickoff from midfield. Each team defends the two goals on its endline and can score in either of the opponent's goals. The team with possession attacks with four players; opponents defend with two field players and a goalkeeper in each goal. Attackers are limited to two or fewer touches to receive and pass the ball. If a defending player steals the ball, he or she must pass it back to one of the goalkeepers before the team can initiate a counterattack. Otherwise, regular soccer rules apply.

**Scoring:** The team scoring the most goals wins.

**Practice tips:** Emphasize immediate transition from defense to attack and vice versa upon change of possession. Attacking players should move the ball quickly in attempts to unbalance the outnumbered defenders and create passing and shooting lanes. Defending players must position to defend the most critical space and attempt to force attackers to shoot from poor (wide) angles.

# 83 Counterattack Numbers-Up (5 v 3)

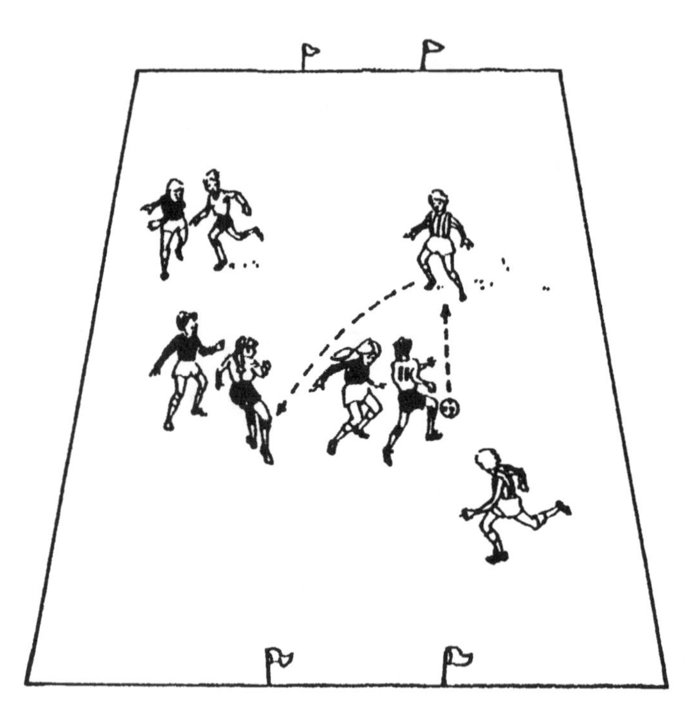

**Minutes:** 15 to 20

**Players:** 8 (2 teams of 3; 2 neutral players)

**Objectives:** To coordinate group tactics in attack and defense; to initiate quick counterattack; to develop endurance

**Setup:** Use markers to create a 30-yard by 50-yard field. Position flags to create a goal 4 yards wide at the midpoint of each endline. Organize two teams of three players each, and have two additional players as neutrals. Use colored vests to differentiate teams and neutral players. No goalkeepers. You'll need one ball per game.

**Procedure:** Begin with a kickoff from the center of the area. Neutral players join the team with the ball to create a 5 v 3 player advantage for the attack. Teams score by kicking the ball through the opponent's goal. A defending player who wins the ball must pass to one of the neutrals in order to initiate the counterattack. Otherwise, regular soccer rules apply.

**Scoring:** The team scoring the most goals wins.

**Practice tips:** Emphasize immediate transition from defense to attack and vice versa upon change of possession. Advanced players can use regulation-size goals and goalkeepers. Reduce the area size for younger players.

# 84 Double-Zone Soccer

**Minutes:** 20 to 25

**Players:** 12 (2 teams of 5; 2 goalkeepers)

**Objectives:** To develop group attack and defense tactics employed in a 3 v 2 situation; to provide goalkeeper training

**Setup:** Use markers to create a 35-yard by 50-yard field area, bisected by a midline. Position a regulation goal at each end of the field. Form two teams of six. Designate three players as attackers, two as defenders, and one as the goalkeeper for each team. Attackers station in the opponent's half of the field, defenders station in their own half, and a goalkeeper stations within the goal, creating a 3 v 2 advantage for the attack in each half. Use colored vests to differentiate teams. You'll need one ball per game. Place an extra supply of balls in each goal.

**Procedure:** Begin with a kickoff from midfield. Each team defends a goal and can score in the opponent's goal. Players are restricted to movement within their assigned half of the field. A defender who steals the ball must pass to a teammate stationed in the opponent's half of the field to initiate the counterattack. After making a save, the goalkeeper distributes directly to a teammate stationed in the opponent's half of the field. After a goal, the team scored against gains possession of the ball. Regular soccer rules apply.

**Scoring:** The team scoring the most goals wins.

**Practice tips:** Because defending players are outnumbered in their zone, they can't use a one-on-one marking scheme. Zonal concepts apply. One defender pressures the player with the ball, while the second defender positions to provide cover for the first defender. Defenders must reposition quickly in response to movement of the ball and opponents. Attackers should use quick passing combinations coupled with off-the-ball support movement to free the extra attacker for a strike on goal.

# 85 Attacking Numbers-Down

**Minutes:** 20

**Players:** 8 (3 teams of 2; 1 neutral player; 1 goalkeeper)

**Objectives:** To develop the team play used when attacking in a numbers-down (fewer players) situation; to develop shooting skills under game-simulated pressures; to develop endurance

**Setup:** Play on one end of a regulation field with a full-size goal centered on the endline. Form three teams of two players each. Station all teams within the penalty area, along with a neutral player who plays with the team in possession. Use colored vests to differentiate teams. The goalkeeper positions within the goal. You'll need one ball per game; place extra balls within the goal.

**Procedure:** The goalkeeper begins play by tossing the ball outside the penalty area, where all three teams vie for possession. The team winning the ball attacks the goal; the other two teams defend. The neutral player joins the team in possession to create a 3 v 4 attacking situation. If a defending player steals the ball, his or her team immediately switches to attack and tries to score. The goalkeeper attempts to save all shots. After a goal or goalkeeper save or if the ball goes out of play, the goalkeeper continues play by tossing the ball outside of the penalty area, where teams again vie for possession.

**Scoring:** Award 1 point for a shot on goal and 2 points for a goal scored. The team scoring the most points wins.

**Practice tips:** The outnumbered (3 v 4) attacking team should attempt to isolate defending players by using one- and two-touch passes combined with creative dribbling. The give-and-go (wall) pass is also an effective tactic when attacking numbers-down.

# 86 Give-and-Go to Score

**Minutes:** 25

**Players:** 9 (2 teams of 3; 1 neutral player; 2 goalkeepers)

**Objectives:** To create scoring opportunities against a packed defense; to improve shooting technique; to develop passing combinations used to penetrate a packed defense

**Setup:** Play on one end of a regulation field. Use markers to extend the penalty area to twice its length, creating a field area 36 yards long and 44 yards wide. Position a full-size goal on each endline. Form two three-player teams, plus a neutral player who plays with the team in possession to provide a 4 v 3 player advantage for the attack. Use colored vests to differentiate teams. Position a goalkeeper in each goal. You'll need one ball per game. Store additional balls within the goals to use as needed. Give one team possession of the ball to begin.

**Procedure:** Each team defends a goal and can score in the opponent's goal. Basic soccer rules apply except that points are scored only from first-time shots originating off a give-and-go (one-two) passing combination. Change of possession occurs after a goal is scored or when the ball travels over the endline or sideline.

**Scoring:** Award 1 point for a shot on goal saved by the goalkeeper and 2 points for a goal scored. All shots must originate off a give-and-go pass. The team scoring the most points wins.

**Practice tips:** The quick give-and-go combination is an effective way to create the space needed to free an attacker for a shot on goal. This game is not appropriate for younger players who lack the skill and tactical awareness to execute the give-and-go pass.

# 87 Pressure and Cover

**Minutes:** 16-20

**Players:** 6

**Objectives:** To coordinate movement of the first (pressuring) and second (covering) defenders; to develop individual tackling skills

**Setup:** Use markers to create a 20- by 25-yard field. Station two defenders in the center. Position one attacker at the midpoint of each sideline. Station a server (coach) outside the grid with an ample supply of balls.

**Procedure:** The server passes a ball to one of the attackers. The player receiving the ball attempts to dribble through the grid to the opposite sideline. The two defenders deny penetration; the first pressures the attacker, while the second provides support. If the attacker cannot immediately penetrate into the space behind the defenders, he or she passes to one of the attackers. Upon receiving the ball, that player immediately attempts to dribble to the opposite sideline. Defenders must immediately readjust position to deny penetration by the new attacker. If the ball is dispossessed by a defender or kicked out of the grid, the server immediately plays another ball to an attacker. An attacker who successfully dribbles to the opposite sideline is awarded 1 point; he or she then returns to original position by running along the outside of the grid. Play for four minutes, and then designate two new defenders. Each player should take a turn as a defender.

**Scoring:** Award 1 point to an attacker who dribbles to an opposite sideline. The attacker scoring the most points wins the game.

**Practice tips:** Emphasize pressure on the ball by the first defender and close cover by the second. Defenders must quickly readjust positions when the ball is played to a different attacker. Attackers stationed on the sidelines can move along the line to make themselves available to receive a pass from the player with the ball when that player cannot penetrate the defense.

# 88 5 v 4 (+ 4) Possession

**Minutes:** 20

**Players:** 13

**Objectives:** To maintain possession of the ball using dribbling and passing combinations; to defend as a unit using pressure, cover, and balance

**Setup:** Use markers to create a 20-yard by 30-yard field. Designate a team of five defenders and a team of four attackers; the remaining four players are neutral. Station attackers and defenders within the area; neutral players station on the perimeter of the area, one on each sideline. Station a server (coach) outside the area with a supply of balls. The defending team has the ball to begin.

**Procedure:** The defending team tries to keep the ball from the attackers within the field area. Defenders are limited to three or fewer touches to receive and pass the ball, and are permitted to pass to neutrals as well as to their teammates. Neutral players are permitted to move laterally along the sidelines and are restricted to two-touches to receive and pass the ball. Neutral players may not pass the ball to another neutral player. When an attacker steals the ball, the attacking team attempts to keep possession. Because attackers are outnumbered, they do not have a touch restriction; they can use whatever means necessary (passing combinations, individual dribbling skills, shielding skills) to maintain possession of the ball. Attackers may *not* use the neutral players for support. If the ball goes out of the field area, the server immediately sends another ball into play. Neutral players switch roles with attackers every five minutes or so.

**Scoring:** The defending team scores 1 point for six or more consecutive passes without a loss of possession. Attackers score 1 point for possessing the ball for 30 seconds or more at a stretch.

**Practice tips:** Emphasize pressure, cover, and balance in defense; focus on individual ball possession skills on attack.

# 89 Front Door, Back Door

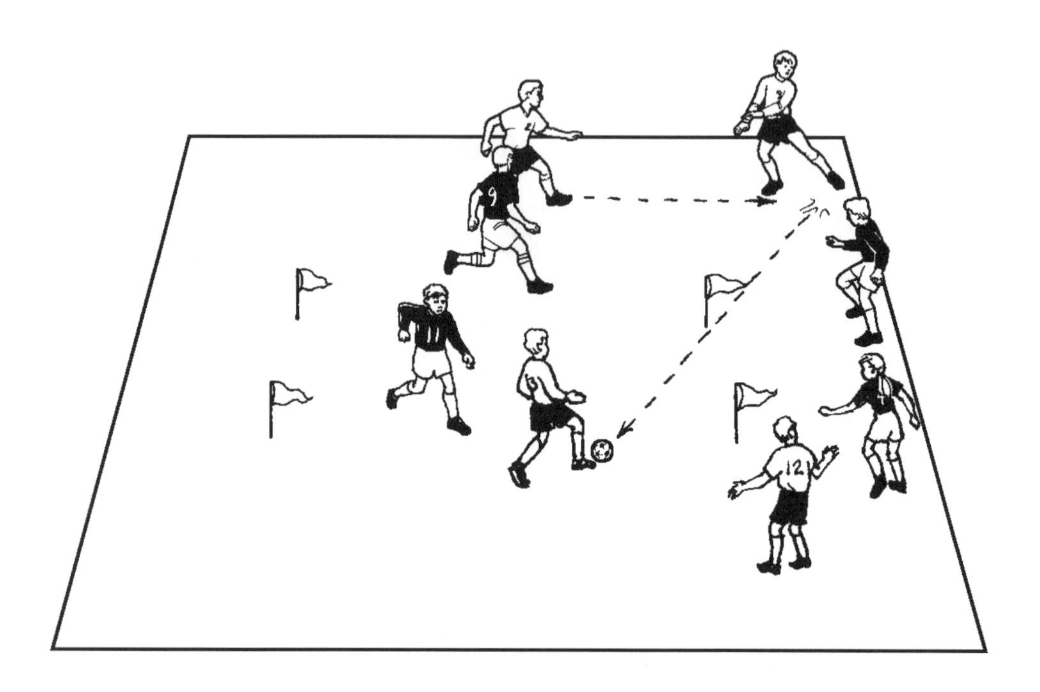

**Minutes:** 15 to 20

**Players:** 6 to 10 (2 equal-sized teams of 3 to 5)

**Objectives:** To develop effective passing combinations and off-the-ball player movement; to improve general endurance

**Setup:** Use markers to create a 30-yard by 40-yard field. Position flags to represent a goal 4 yards wide in each half of the field, about 10 yards in from the endlines. Form two teams of equal numbers. Use colored vests to differentiate teams. No goalkeepers. You'll need one ball per game.

**Procedure:** Begin with a kickoff from the center of the area. Regular soccer rules apply, except that goals can be scored through either goal. In addition, shots may be scored from either side of the goals, through the "back door" or the "front door."

**Scoring:** The team scoring the most goals wins.

**Practice tips:** Require a tight one-on-one marking scheme to reduce the time and space available. Stress the importance of immediate transition between defense and attack upon change of possession. Add restrictions when applicable (such as limited number of touches).

# 90 Half-Court Soccer

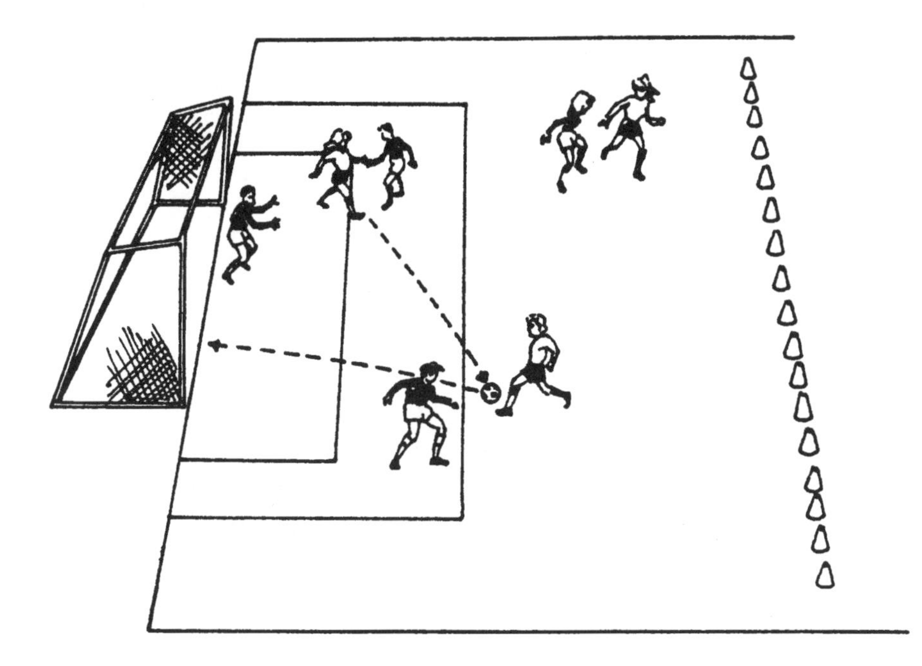

**Minutes:** 25

**Players:** 7 (2 teams of 3; 1 neutral goalkeeper)

**Objectives:** To coordinate group tactics used in attack and defense; to improve fitness; to provide goalkeeper training

**Setup:** Play on one end of a regulation field with a full-size goal centered on the endline. Position a line of markers 35 yards from the goal, spanning the width of the field. Organize two teams of three players each. Use colored vests to differentiate teams. Station one team outside the 35-yard zone with the ball. The opposing team positions to defend the goal. The goalkeeper positions within the goal.

**Procedure:** The team with the ball enters the defending (35-yard) zone to attack the goal; their opponents defend. Change of possession occurs when the ball goes out of play, a goal is scored, the goalkeeper makes a save, or a defender steals the ball. Each new attack must begin outside the 35-yard zone. Teams alternate playing on attack and defense, depending on which has possession of the ball. Otherwise, regular soccer rules apply.

**Scoring:** Award 2 points for each goal scored and 1 point for a shot on goal saved by the keeper. The team scoring the most points wins.

**Practice tips:** Virtually all group tactical concepts can be demonstrated in a 3 v 3 situation. Emphasize the attacking concepts of width, depth, and penetration. Emphasize the defensive principles of pressure (first defender), cover (second defender), and balance (third defender).

# 91 Numbers-Up Scoring (3 v 2 to 2 v 1)

**Minutes:** 20 to 25

**Players:** 14 (2 teams of 6; 2 goalkeepers)

**Objectives:** To improve group attack; to defend when outnumbered

**Setup:** Play on a 30-yard by 30-yard field with a full-size goal centered on each endline (goals A and B). Station a goalkeeper in each goal. Divide the remaining players into two teams (team 1 and team 2) of six players each. Use colored vests to differentiate teams. Position both teams on the same endline of the field, one team to each side of goal A. Team 1 has the ball to begin. Position two players from team 2 to defend goal B. Place a supply of balls inside each goal.

**Procedure:** Three players from team 1 advance off the endline to attack goal B, defended by two players from team 2 and a goalkeeper. Immediately after a shot on goal, a shot traveling over the endline, or a ball stolen by a defender, the goalkeeper in goal B distributes a ball to the original two defenders (team 2), who immediately attack goal A. One of the three original attackers from team 1 plays as a single defender, creating a 2 v 1 player advantage for team 2 as they counterattack goal A. The other two attackers from team 1 remain near the endline (goal B) to defend goal B in the next round.

Immediately after a shot on goal A, three players from team 2 advance off the line to attack goal B, which is now defended by two players from team 1. The game continues back and forth, with teams attacking goal B 3 v 2 and counterattacking goal A 2 v 1.

**Scoring:** Award 1 point for each goal scored. The team scoring the most goals wins the game.

**Practice tips:** Emphasize immediate transition from attack to defense and vice versa.

# 92 Team Attack and Defend (7 v 5)

**Minutes:** 25 to 30

**Players:** 13 (7 attackers; 5 defenders; 1 goalkeeper)

**Objective:** To develop team tactics used in attack and defense

**Setup:** Play on half a regulation field with a full-size goal centered on the endline. Position cones or flags to represent two mini-goals (3 yards wide) 20 yards apart on the halfway line. Designate a team of seven to play against a team of five and a goalkeeper. Use colored vests to differentiate teams. The goalkeeper stations in the regulation goal; there are no goalkeepers in the mini-goals. You'll need one ball per game. An extra supply of balls is recommended.

**Procedure:** Organize the seven-player team with two strikers and five midfielders. Organize the five-player team with four defenders and a defensive midfielder fronting the defense. The seven-player team attempts to score in the regulation goal and defends the mini-goals. The five-player team gains possession by intercepting passes, tackling the ball away from an opponent, or receiving the ball from the goalkeeper after a save or a goal. The five-player team can score through either of the small goals on the halfway line. Play is continuous.

**Scoring:** The seven-player team scores 2 points for a goal and 1 point for a shot on goal saved by the goalkeeper. The five-player team scores 1 point by kicking the ball through either of the small goals. The team scoring the most points wins.

**Practice tips:** The five-player team, being outnumbered, must position to protect the most central areas from which goals are most likely to be scored. Impose restrictions to make the game more challenging for the seven-player team (such as two- or three-touch passing only) or to emphasize specific aspects of attacking and defending tactics.

# 93 Dribble the Endline

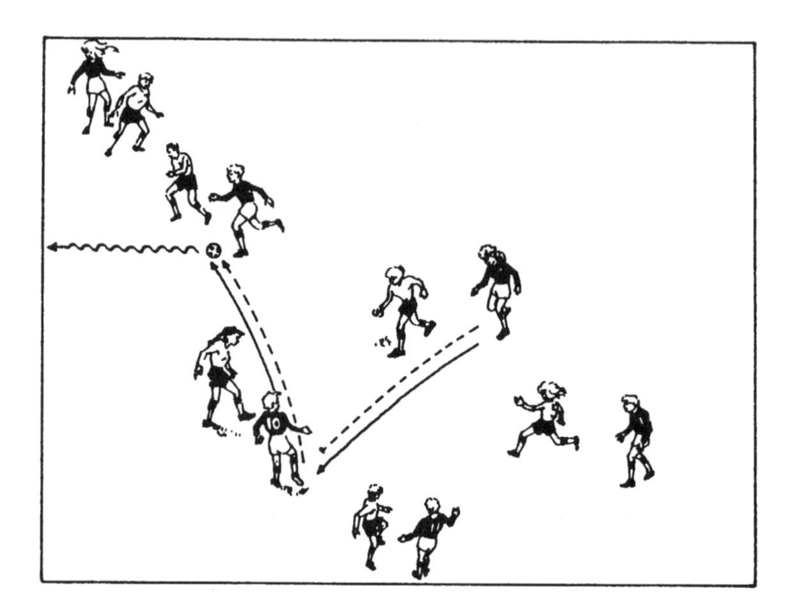

**Minutes:** 25

**Players:** 12 to 16 (in 2 equal-sized teams)

**Objectives:** To coordinate team attack and defense tactics; to improve player ability to compete in 1 v 1 situations; to develop individual dribbling, shielding, and tackling skills

**Setup:** Use markers to create a 50-yard by 70-yard field. Organize two teams of equal size. Station one team in each half of the field. Use colored vests to differentiate teams. You'll need one ball per game.

**Procedure:** Begin with a kickoff from the center of the field. Except for the scoring, regular soccer rules are in effect. Goals are scored by dribbling the ball across the opponent's endline rather than by shooting. The entire length of the endline is considered the goal line. There are no goalkeepers.

**Scoring:** Teams score 1 point for dribbling the ball across the opponent's endline. The team scoring the most points wins.

**Practice tips:** Require one-on-one defensive marking, with each player assigned a specific opponent. Players should take on (attempt to dribble past) opponents only in certain situations and areas of the field. Encourage players to take on opponents in the attacking third of the field, nearest to the opponent's endline. Beating an opponent on the dribble in that area will create a scoring opportunity, so the risk of possession loss is more than compensated by the potential benefit. Discourage players from taking on opponents via the dribble in the team's defending third (the part of the field nearest the endline), where possession loss might lead to a goal against the team.

# 94 Three Zone End-to-End

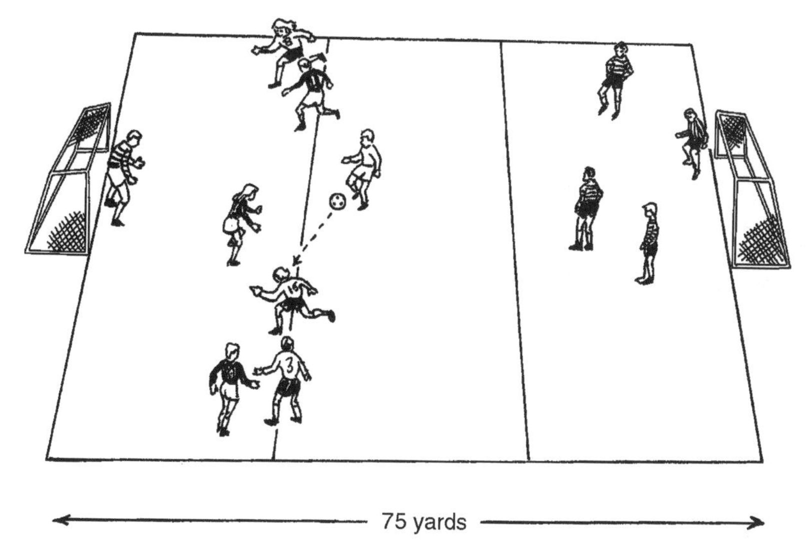


**Minutes:** 25

**Players:** 12 (3 teams of 3; 1 neutral player; 2 goalkeepers)

**Objectives:** To develop group attack and defense tactics; to improve endurance

**Setup:** Form three teams (A, B, C) of three players each. Designate an additional player as a neutral attacker. Use markers to create a 40-yard by 75-yard field. Position a regulation goal on each endline. Divide the field into three 40-yard by 25-yard zones. Station team A in the middle zone with the ball. Teams B and C station in opposite end zones. Station a goalkeeper in each goal. The neutral player joins the team in possession (team A). Use colored vests to differentiate teams.

**Procedure:** Team A, assisted by the neutral player, moves forward out of the middle zone to attack one of the goals. The defending team gains the ball when a pass is intercepted, when the goalkeeper makes a save, when a goal is scored, or when the ball travels over the endline last touched by the attacking team. Upon change of possession, the original defending team moves into the middle zone, organizes, and then attacks the opposite goal. The team losing possession (team A) remains in the end zone to defend the goal in the next round of play. The neutral player always joins the team with the ball to produce a 4 v 3 player advantage for the attack. Play is continuous as teams attack one goal and then the other.

**Scoring:** The team scoring the most goals wins.

**Practice tips:** Upon gaining possession of the ball, the team should sprint from its end zone into the middle zone, quickly organize themselves, and then attack the opposite goal. In actual match situations, any delay in the attack allows additional defenders time to recover to offset the numerical advantage.

# 95 No Tackle

**Minutes:** 25

**Players:** 10 to 16 (2 equal-sized teams of 4 to 7; 2 goalkeepers)

**Objectives:** To develop group passing combinations and proper support movement; to improve defensive organization; to read the game and anticipate the actions of opponents

**Setup:** Form two teams of equal numbers. Use markers to create a 40-yard by 60-yard field area with a full-size goal centered on each endline. Station teams in opposite halves of the field, with a goalkeeper in each goal. Use colored vests to differentiate teams. One team has the ball to begin.

**Procedure:** Commence with a kickoff from the center of the field. Limit players to three or fewer touches to receive, pass, and shoot the ball. Defending players gain possession only by intercepting passes or when the attacking team plays the ball out of bounds. Tackling the ball from an opponent is not allowed. Teams switch from attack to defense and vice versa on change of possession.

**Scoring:** Points are scored by players kicking the ball through the opponent's goal. The team scoring the most points wins.

**Practice tips:** Defending players must anticipate the action of opponents and position to block passing lanes and intercept passes. Reduce the area size for highly skilled players to reduce the time available for decision-making and skill execution. Allow beginning players five or fewer touches to pass and receive the ball.

# 96 Tactical Dribbling

**Minutes:** 20

**Players:** 10 to 12 (2 equal-sized teams of 4 or 5; 2 goalkeepers)

**Objectives:** To encourage appropriate use of dribbling skills in game situations; to develop endurance

**Setup:** Use markers to create a 40-yard by 60-yard field with a regulation goal centered on each endline. Divide the field lengthwise into three 20- by 40-yard zones. Organize two teams of equal numbers. Station a goalkeeper in each goal. Use colored vests to differentiate teams. One ball is required per game; an extra supply of balls is recommended.

**Procedure:** Begin with a kickoff from the center of the field. Each team defends a goal and can score in the opponent's goal. Regular soccer rules are in effect except for the following: (1) players may use at most two touches to pass and receive the ball when in the defending third of the field nearest their goal; (2) in the middle zone, players may dribble to advance the ball when in open space but can't take on and beat opponents; and (3) in the attacking third of the field, players must beat at least one opponent on the dribble before passing to a teammate or shooting on goal. Violating the zone restrictions results in a loss of possession to the opposing team.

**Scoring:** The team scoring the most goals wins.

**Practice tips:** Dribbling skills are used most effectively in the attacking third of the field, an area where the risk of possession loss is outweighed by the possibility of creating a goal scoring opportunity. Discourage excessive dribbling in the defending and middle zones, as these are areas where loss of possession might mean scoring opportunities for the opponent.

# 97 Possession With a Purpose

**Minutes:** 25

**Players:** 10 (2 teams of 4; 2 goalkeepers)

**Objectives:** To maintain possession of the ball from opponents; to coordinate group attack and defense tactics; to improve fitness

**Setup:** Use markers to create a 30-yard by 40-yard playing area, with a full-size goal centered on each endline. Form players into two teams of equal number, plus goalkeepers. Use colored vests to differentiate teams. You'll need one ball.

**Procedure:** Begin with a kickoff from the center of the field. Each team defends a goal. Teams score by kicking the ball through the opponent's goal or by completing eight consecutive passes without a possession loss. The defending team can win the ball by intercepting passes or tackling the ball from opponents. Except for the method of scoring, regular soccer rules apply.

**Scoring:** Award 1 point for a goal scored and 2 points for eight consecutive passes. The team scoring the most points wins.

**Practice tips:** Teams should demonstrate patience in organizing their attack while looking for opportunities to penetrate the opponent's defense for a strike at goal. Toward that aim, the team with the ball should try to maintain possession until there is an opportunity to move forward and score. This tactic also commits defenders to the area of the ball, which creates space within and behind the defense for the attacking team to exploit.

# 98 Four Goals

**Minutes:** 25

**Players:** 18 (2 teams of 6; 4 goalkeepers; 2 neutral players)

**Objectives:** To change the point of attack to relieve defensive pressure; to develop effective counterattack combinations; to improve physical endurance

**Setup:** Use markers to create a 60-yard by 75-yard field. Place two full-size goals on each endline, about 25 yards apart. Station one team in each half of the field. Put a goalkeeper in each goal. Use colored vests to differentiate teams. One team has the ball to begin.

**Procedure:** Each team defends the two goals on its endline and can score in the opponent's two goals. Neutral players join the team with possession to create a two-player advantage for the attack. Otherwise, regular soccer rules are in effect.

**Scoring:** The team scoring the most goals wins.

**Practice tips:** Encourage players to attack the most vulnerable (least defended) goal. They do so by quickly switching the point of attack to expose the opponent's weaknesses. To make the game more challenging, impose restrictions on advanced players (such as limiting to two-touches to pass and receive the ball).

# 99 Tight Marking

**Minutes:** 25

**Players:** 10 to 16

**Objectives:** To improve one-on-one marking; to coordinate group attack and defense; to develop endurance

**Setup:** Organize two teams of equal number. Use markers to create a 50-yard by 75-yard field. Position flags to form a goal four yards wide centered on each endline. Use colored vests to differentiate teams. No goalkeepers. You'll need one ball per game.

**Procedure:** Begin with a kickoff from the center of the field. Each team defends a goal. Require strict one-on-one marking of all players. Because there are no goalkeepers, and shots can be taken from anywhere on the field, defensive marking must be very tight to close passing lanes and prevent long-range goals. Change of possession occurs when a defender steals the ball, the ball goes out of play, or a goal is scored.

**Scoring:** A ball kicked through the goal below the height of the flag counts as a goal scored. The team scoring the most goals wins.

**Practice tips:** Defending players use tight marking to limit the time and space available to opponents. Reduce the field size for highly skilled players. As a variation, place three small goals along each endline to provide additional scoring options.

# 100 Neutral Wingers

**Minutes:** 25

**Players:** 12 (2 teams of 4; 2 neutral wingers; 2 goalkeepers)

**Objectives:** To develop effective flank play; to improve your team's ability to score off crossed balls; to defend serves into the goal area

**Setup:** Use markers to create a 40-yard by 60-yard field area, with a full-size goal centered on each endline. Mark a channel 5 yards wide on each flank, extending the length of the field. Organize two teams of four players. Use colored vests to differentiate teams. Designate two additional players as neutral wingers, one in each flank channel. Station a goalkeeper in each goal. You'll need one ball per game. Have an extra supply of balls behind each goal.

**Procedure:** Teams play 4 v 4 in the 30-yard-wide middle channel. Each team defends a goal and can score in the opponent's goal. The wingers join the team with possession to create a 6 v 4 player advantage for the attacking team. Goals can be scored directly from shots originating in the middle channel or from balls crossed into the goal area by the wingers. Wingers are restricted to movement within their flank channel. When a winger receives the ball from a central player or the goalkeeper, he or she then dribbles toward the opponent's endline and crosses the ball into the goal area. Otherwise, regular soccer rules apply.

**Scoring:** Award 1 point for each goal scored from a shot originating within the middle channel, and 2 points for a goal scored directly off a crossed ball. The team scoring the most points wins.

**Practice tips:** This game reinforces the use of flank play to open up an opponent's defense. It also provides training for the goalkeeper in handling crossed balls.

# 101 Multiple Scoring Options

**Minutes:** 25

**Players:** 12 (2 teams of 5; 2 goalkeepers)

**Objectives:** To coordinate attack and defense tactics used in small-group situations; to improve general endurance

**Setup:** Use markers to create a 50-yard by 75-yard field area, with a full-size goal centered on each endline. Place flags to create a mini-goal two yards wide on each flank near the halfway line. Station teams in opposite halves of the field, with a goalkeeper in each goal. Use colored vests to differentiate teams. You'll need one ball per game.

**Procedure:** Begin with a kickoff from the center of the field. Teams score points by dribbling through either of the small flank goals, by shooting the ball past the opposing goalkeeper through the large goal, or by combining with teammates for eight consecutive passes. Other than the method of scoring, regular soccer rules apply.

**Scoring:** Award 3 points for a goal scored in the regulation goal and 2 points for eight consecutive passes without loss of possession. Award 1 point for dribbling through a flank goal. The team scoring the most points wins.

**Practice tips:** Encourage players to choose the best scoring option under the circumstances. For example, they should possess the ball (make consecutive passes) to draw opponents to them, then attack the goal once they've committed the defender(s).

# 102 Quick Counter

**Minutes:** 25 to 30

**Players:** 18 (9-player team; 7-player team; 2 goalkeepers)

**Objectives:** To develop effective transition play in attack and defense; to practice group and team attack and defense tactics

**Setup:** Play on a regulation field with a full-size goal on each endline. Place a line of markers the width of the field 35 yards from each endline, forming three field zones. Organize a team of nine and a team of seven. Station one team in each half and a goalkeeper in each goal. Use colored vests to differentiate teams. You'll need at least one ball, and an extra supply of balls is recommended.

**Procedure:** Begin with a kickoff from center field. Each team defends a goal and may score in the opponent's goal. Regular soccer rules apply, except for one variation: the nine-player team must use three or fewer touches to pass and receive the ball. The seven-player team has no touch restriction. As coach, you or one of your assistants should referee. Every few minutes, stop play and award the seven-player team a free kick from their half of the field; this allows them to play a long pass over the top of the nine-player team. When the free kick is taken, all defending players should station in the middle field zone. Defending players can't react to the ball until a player from the seven-player team touches it. At this point, defending players must immediately track back to thwart a counterattack.

**Scoring:** Award 1 point for a shot on goal saved by the goalkeeper and 2 points for a goal scored. The team scoring the most points wins.

**Practice tips:** Teammates move forward quickly as a compact unit to mount an effective counterattack. Defending players must make swift and direct recovery runs to defend the counter.

# 103 Defend Your Zone

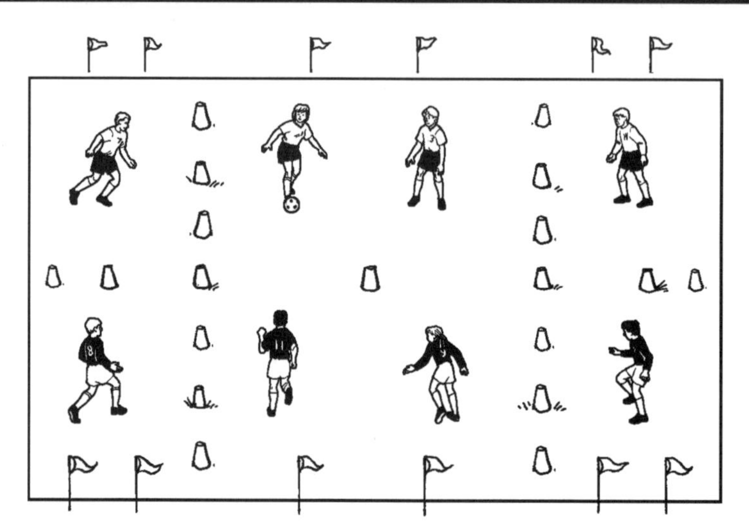

**Minutes:** 15 to 20

**Players:** 8 (2 teams of 4)

**Objectives:** To practice zonal defense concepts; to develop proper defensive shape

**Setup:** Use markers to create a 20-yard by 35-yard area. Use additional markers to divide the area into three zones. The end zones (1 and 3) are 10 yards wide by 20 yards long; the middle zone (2) is 15 yards wide by 20 yards long. Place cones or flags to represent a small goal (2 yards wide) on opposite endlines of each zone. Divide the entire area horizontally by placing a line of markers through the middle of the field, creating six smaller areas. You'll need one ball per game. Use colored vests to differentiate teams.

**Procedure:** Organize two teams of four. Each team is responsible for defending three goals and may score in the opponent's three goals. One player from each team stations in zones 1 and 3. These players defend the team's goal in these zones. Two players from each team station in zone 2 and are responsible for defending the goal in that zone. Defending players are restricted to movement within their zone. There are no restrictions on the team with the ball; attacking players can move between zones if they want to. Otherwise, regular soccer rules apply.

**Scoring:** Award 1 point for each goal scored.

**Practice tips:** As a variation, allow players stationed in the middle zone to slide sideways into an end zone to provide support (defensive cover) for the teammate in that zone. Likewise, allow defending players stationed in the end zones to slide laterally into the middle zone to provide cover and balance for the central defenders. Emphasize proper defensive shape and balance. Zonal positioning is based on location of the ball and position of defending teammates, *not* on the position of opposing players.

# 104 Sideline Neutrals

**Minutes:** 20 to 25

**Players:** 20 (3 teams of 6; 2 goalkeepers)

**Objective:** To use the width and depth of the field to exploit an outnumbered defending side

**Setup:** Use markers to create a 40-yard by 60-yard field with a full-size goal centered on each endline. Teams A and B station within the field area; each team defends a goal. Team C players station along the perimeter of the field as neutral support players, one on each sideline and two along each endline. Use colored vests to differentiate teams. Put a goalkeeper in each goal.

**Procedure:** Teams A and B compete against each other. Players can use the sideline and endline neutral players (team C) as passing options when in possession of the ball, creating an 12 v 6 player advantage for the attack. Neutral players may not enter the field area—they can move only laterally along the perimeter lines. Sideline neutrals have a two-touch restriction, and endline neutrals have a one-touch restriction. Play for 10 minutes or until two goals are scored (whichever comes first), after which one of the middle teams (A or B) becomes the neutral players and team C moves into the middle of the field. Play several rounds.

**Scoring:** Award 1 point for a goal scored. The team scoring the most goals wins.

**Practice tips:** The attacking team should use the neutral players to create scoring opportunities. Players should vary the type and distance of their passes, including long passes behind the opposing defense to the neutral players stationed on the endlines. Impose restrictions (two-touch, three-touch, etc.) depending on the age and ability of players.

# 105 Linking the Team

**Minutes:** 20 to 25

**Players:** 18 (2 teams of 8; 2 goalkeepers)

**Objectives:** To develop total team support when advancing from the defending into the attacking thirds of the field; to coordinate group passing combinations

**Setup:** Play on a 65-yard by 75-yard field divided lengthwise into three 25-yard zones. Position a full-size goal at the midpoint of each endline. Form two teams (team 1 and team 2) of eight players each. Each team positions three players in its defending third, three players in the middle third, and two players in the attacking third nearest to the opponent's goal. Use colored vests to differentiate teams. A goalkeeper stations in each goal. The team 1 goalkeeper has the ball to begin.

**Procedure:** To begin play, the goalkeeper distributes the ball to a teammate stationed within the team's defensive third of the field. Players advance the ball by dribbling into the middle zone or by completing a pass to a teammate stationed in the middle zone, after which one player stationed in the defensive third moves forward and enters the middle zone, creating a 4 v 3 player advantage in that zone. The four teammates in the middle zone try to maintain possession and pass the ball to a teammate stationed in the attacking third, after which one player from the middle third moves forward to create a 3 v 3 player situation in the attacking third. Defending players must remain in their assigned zones. Teams reverse roles on change of possession or after a goal is scored. Regular soccer rules are in effect.

**Scoring:** Award 1 point for a goal scored. The team scoring the most points wins.

**Practice tips:** Teams should play it safe in their defending third, an area where possession loss can prove costly. Players can afford to take greater risks in the attacking third of the field, where loss of possession is not so critical. Impose restrictions to emphasize specific concepts or to make the activity more difficult. For example, you might limit players to two-touches in their defending third, three-touches in the middle third, and unlimited touches in the attacking third.

# 106 Stretching the Field

**Minutes:** 20 to 30

**Players:** 20 (2 teams of 9; 2 goalkeepers)

**Objectives:** To create gaps of open space within the opponent's defense; to play direct, from back to front, using accurate passes over distance

**Setup:** Play on a regulation field with a full-size goal centered on each endline. Use markers to designate an "offside line" 30 yards from each endline. Position teams on opposite halves of the field. Use colored vests to differentiate teams. You'll need one ball.

**Procedure:** Begin with a kickoff from the center spot. Regular soccer rules apply, except for a variation of the offside rule. A player stationed beyond the offside line (30 yards or more from goal) is not considered offside, even if he or she is behind the last defender. This rule variation prevents the defending team from compressing the field and enables the attacking team to play the ball behind defending players.

**Scoring:** Use regular scoring.

**Practice tips:** Encourage teams to take advantage of the liberal offside rule. When possible, back players should look to play the ball into their deep-lying targets. As a variation, limit players to two touches in their own half of the field. This encourages quick ball movement and more direct play.

# 107 Breakaway and Score

**Minutes:** 20 to 30

**Players:** 16 (2 teams of 7; 2 goalkeepers)

**Objective:** To create breakaway situations

**Setup:** Play on a regulation field with a full-size goal on each endline. Use markers to designate two 5-yard deep neutral zones spanning the width of the field, one in each half, about 25 yards from the halfway line. Organize two teams of seven players. Use colored vests to differentiate teams. Both teams station in the central zone (between the neutral zones). Station a goalkeeper in each goal. Place a supply of balls outside one of the sidelines. Award one team possession of a ball to begin.

**Procedure:** Begin with a kickoff at center field. The team with possession attempts to advance the ball into their opponent's five-yard deep neutral zone, either via a completed pass or dribbling. Defending players try to prevent opponents from advancing the ball into their neutral zone but can't actually enter the zone. Teams reverse roles on each change of possession. Once the ball had been advanced into a neutral zone, the player with the ball proceeds at top speed toward the goal in a breakaway situation. One player from the defending team is allowed to give chase. After each breakaway situation, restart play with a kickoff from center field. Regular soccer rules are in effect except for the method of scoring.

**Scoring:** Award 1 point for each goal scored off a breakaway situation. The team scoring the most points wins the game.

**Practice tips:** The attacking team must possess the ball while searching for opportunities to penetrate the opponent's neutral zone. Defending players should use the universal defensive principles of pressure, cover, and balance to block passing lanes and deny penetration.

# Part VI

# Goalkeeper Training Games

The goalkeeper is arguably the single most important member of the soccer team, the player whose primary responsibility is and always will be to keep the ball out of the net. It is somewhat surprising then that the keeper is also the player most often neglected during training sessions. In all too many instances the goalkeeper spends the bulk of practice time standing in the goal with explicit orders to "stop all shots." Obviously that is not sufficient training for the team's last line of defense, the final barrier preventing an opponent's score. The keeper is a specialist and must be trained as such.

The goalkeeper is the only player on the team permitted use of the hands to control the ball, and must perform a unique set of skills that differ in many respects from those used by the field players. The keeper must be proficient at receiving low, medium, and high balls, diving to save, distributing the ball by throwing or kicking, and saving breakaways. He or she must also develop a thorough mastery of angle play (positioning) and team tactics. The practice games described in this part are most appropriate for intermediate and advanced players who have previously been introduced to basic goalkeeper skills. The games can be used effectively to sharpen those skills as well as to supplement more intense goalkeeper training.

**Note:** Players under 12 years of age should not specialize solely in the goalkeeper position. It is important for all players, even those who feel they may ultimately want to be a goalkeeper, to develop the fundamental foot skills used by field players. The constantly changing role of the goalkeeper requires that he or she be able to perform foot skills much more so than in the past.

# 108 Toss and Catch

**Minutes:** 15

**Players:** Unlimited (in pairs)

**Objective:** To develop "soft" hands

**Setup:** Goalkeepers A and B stand approximately four yards apart, facing one another. Each holds a ball in his or her right hand at about head height.

**Procedure:** While slowly shuffling across the width of the field, the keepers simultaneously toss a ball from their right hand to their partner's left hand. Tosses are received on the fingertips with one hand only. Return the ball by tossing it with the left hand to the partner's right hand. Continue shuffling back and forth for 10 widths of the field.

**Scoring:** Assess 1 penalty point each time a goalkeeper drops the ball or makes an inaccurate toss. Each player keeps track of his or her own penalty points. The keeper accumulating the fewest number of points wins.

**Practice tips:** Maintain balance and body control at all times. Players should not cross their legs when shuffling sideways. Make the game more challenging by increasing the velocity of tosses.

# 109 Skippers

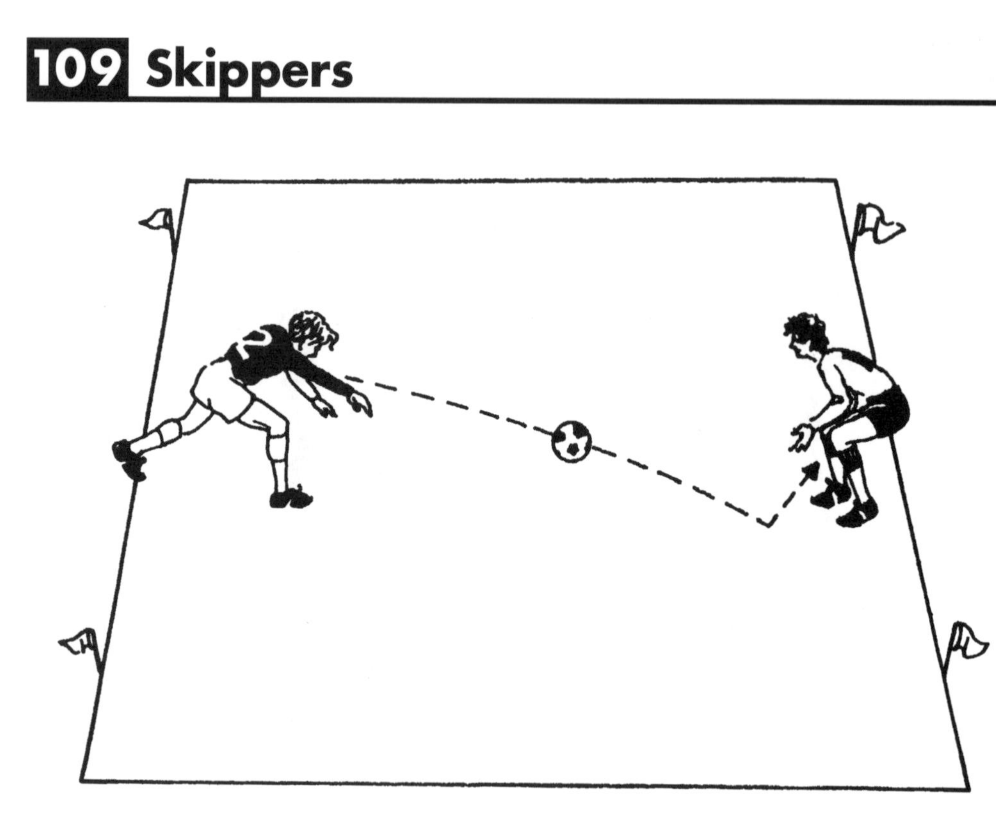

**Minutes:** 15

**Players:** Unlimited (in pairs)

**Objective:** To save low-driven shots using the forward vault technique

**Setup:** Pair goalkeepers (A and B) for competition. Use markers to outline a 15-yard by 20-yard area for each pair. Position flags to represent a 5-yard wide goal on each endline. Station a keeper in each goal. Goalkeeper A has the ball to begin.

**Procedure:** Keeper A throws or half-volleys the ball so that it bounces (skips) off the ground directly in front of B, who attempts to save using the forward vault technique. If keeper B fails to hold the ball, keeper A may follow up the shot and score off the rebound. Keepers take turns attempting to score against each other.

**Scoring:** Award 1 point for a ball held without rebound. The goalkeeper who scores the most points wins.

**Practice tips:** The keeper must be able to secure and hold low-skipping shots, particularly when field conditions are wet and slippery. They must align with the oncoming ball and dive forward to smother the shot, clutching the ball between forearms and chest. Elbows and arms should be cradled underneath the ball to prevent it from bouncing free. Goalkeepers should not try to catch the low-skipping shot directly in their hands, as this increases the risk of a rebound.

# 110 Pingers

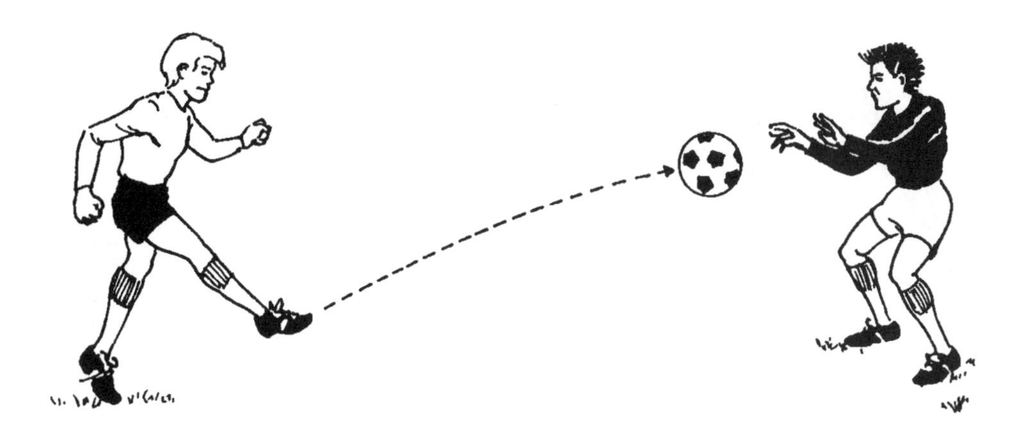

**Minutes:** 10

**Players:** Unlimited (in pairs)

**Objective:** To catch and hold powerful shots

**Setup:** Partners face one another at a distance of about 10 yards. You'll need one ball for this drill.

**Procedure:** Keepers volley ("ping") the ball back and forth to one another. All volley kicks should be aimed at the partner's chest or head; diving to save is not necessary. The ball should be received on the fingertips and palms, with hands extended and head behind the ball. Tell keepers to withdraw their hands on contact with the ball to cushion the impact.

**Scoring:** Award 1 point for each "pinger" that is caught and held without a rebound. The keeper who scores the most points wins.

**Practice tips:** Keepers should position behind the ball as it arrives, to serve as a barrier. Focus on aligning head and hands, with arms extended and slightly flexed at the elbow. Palms should face forward with fingers spread and slightly extended. Keepers should withdraw their hands slightly as the ball arrives to cushion the impact.

# 111 Goalie Wars

**Minutes:** 20

**Players:** Unlimited (in pairs)

**Objective:** To improve shot-saving ability

**Setup:** Pair goalkeepers (A and B) for competition. Use markers to outline a 20-yard by 25-yard field for each pair. Position a full-size portable goal on each endline; if goals aren't available, use flags to represent regulation-width goals. Keepers station in opposite goals. Keeper A has the ball to begin. Place extra balls in each goal.

**Procedure:** Keeper A takes three steps forward off the goal line and attempts to volley or throw the ball past B. Keeper B may move forward off the goal line to narrow the shooting angle. After the save, or goal scored, keeper B tries to score against A in the same manner. Keepers return to their goal line after each shot on goal.

**Scoring:** Award points for preventing goals: 2 points for a save caught and held and 1 point for a save made by deflecting (parrying) the ball wide or over the goal. The keeper who scores the most points wins.

**Practice tips:** Goalkeepers should move forward off the goal line to narrow the shooter's angle. Avoid rebounds. If keepers are not confident of holding the ball, they should deflect (parry) it out of play.

# 112 Save the Breakaway

**Minutes:** 15 to 20

**Players:** Unlimited (in pairs)

**Objective:** To save in a breakaway situation

**Setup:** Goalkeepers (A and B) pair off for competition. Use markers to outline a 20-yard by 25-yard field for each group. Position cones or flags to represent a goal, 8 yards wide, on each endline. Goalkeepers station in opposite goals. Keeper A has the ball to begin.

**Procedure:** A attempts to score against B by dribbling past or passing the ball underneath him or her, simulating a breakaway situation. Shooting is prohibited. Rebounds off the goalkeeper are playable. After each attempt (save or goal scored), goalkeepers return to their goals and repeat the round.

**Scoring:** Award 1 point for each save of a breakaway situation. The keeper who scores the most points wins.

**Practice tips:** The keeper should move forward off the goal line to narrow the shooting angle and present a barrier to the attacker. As he or she advances, the keeper begins to break down into a semi-crouch posture with knees bent and arms extended down to sides. The keeper goes down to the side (not head first) with arms extended toward the ball to make the save.

# 113 Low-Ball Training

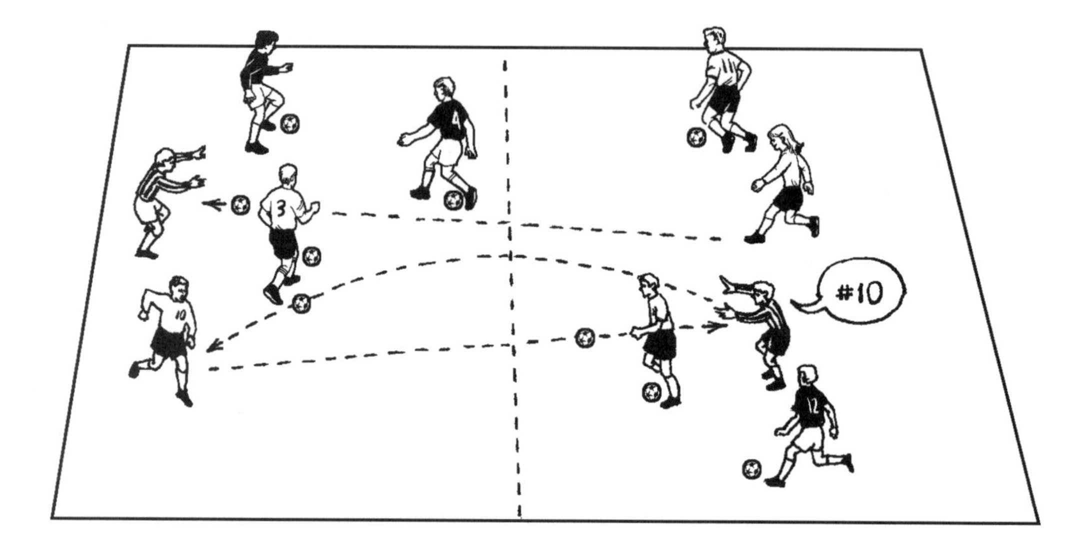


**Minutes:** 10 to 15

**Players:** 10

**Objective:** To improve goalkeepers' ability to receive low- and medium-height balls

**Setup:** Use markers to outline a 30-yard by 60-yard field area, divided by a midline. Station one goalkeeper and four field players in each half of the field. Each field player has a ball.

**Procedure:** Field players dribble a ball within their half of the field area. Every few seconds, the keeper stationed in the opposite half shouts a player's name. That player kicks a low- (ground) or medium-high ball directly at the goalkeeper stationed in the opposite half. The keeper receives the ball using the appropriate technique, returns the ball to the player who kicked it, and then calls for another ball from a different player. Continue for several minutes as keepers receive low- and medium-height balls from field players stationed in the opposite half of the field.

**Scoring:** None

**Practice tips:** The keeper should square his or her body with the server and move forward to meet the ball as it arrives. Field players can vary the service between ground balls and knee-high shots.

# 114 Rapid Fire Shoot and Save

**Minutes:** 15-20

**Players:** 4 (3 shooters; 1 goalkeeper)

**Objective:** To improve shot-saving ability

**Setup:** Play on one end of a regulation field with a full-size goal. Place 12 to 16 balls an equal distance apart on the front edge of the penalty area. Station three shooters about 25 yards from goal. The keeper positions in the goal.

**Procedure:** Shooters alternate attempting to score from a one-time strike of a stationary ball. After each save or score, the next shooter immediately initiates his or her approach to a ball. Allow the keeper just enough time to set in the ready position in preparation for the next shot. Continue shooting until the supply of balls is depleted; then reposition balls for the next round. Play five rounds.

**Scoring:** The goalkeeper gets 1 point for each save. Shooters get 2 points for each goal. The player (goalkeeper or shooters) scoring the most points wins the round.

**Practice tips:** Because the keeper will need to dive repeatedly, he or she should wear appropriate clothing (padded shorts, long-sleeved shirts with padded elbows) to reduce the incidence of bumps and bruises. Reduce the shooting distance for younger players.

# 115 Dive to Save (5 v 2 + 2 v 5)

**Minutes:** 20

**Players:** 16 (2 teams of 7 players; 2 goalkeepers)

**Objective:** To develop shot-saving techniques in a game-simulated environment

**Setup:** Use markers to create a 40-yard by 60-yard field divided by a midline. Position a full-size goal on each endline. Organize two teams of seven. Use colored scrimmage vests to differentiate teams. Each team positions five players in the opponent's half of the field and two players in its own defending half, creating a 5-attacker versus 2-defender situation in each half. Station a goalkeeper in each goal. You'll need one ball per game; place extra balls in each goal. Award one team the ball to begin.

**Procedure:** Goalkeeper initiates play by distributing the ball to a teammate in the opponent's half of the field. Attacking players are permitted only two touches of the ball before they must pass to a teammate or shoot at goal. If a defender wins the ball, or the goalkeeper makes a save, he or she immediately plays the ball to a teammate stationed in the opponent's half of the field. Play for 20 minutes, five attackers versus two defenders in each half. Regular soccer rules apply, other than the touch restriction.

**Scoring:** Goalkeeper conceding the fewest goals wins.

**Practice tips:** This game should produce many scoring opportunities. Goalkeepers must communicate effectively with their outnumbered defenders to compact the most vital space and force opponents to take poor percentage (wide-angle) shots.

# 116 Multiple Gate Shoot-and-Save

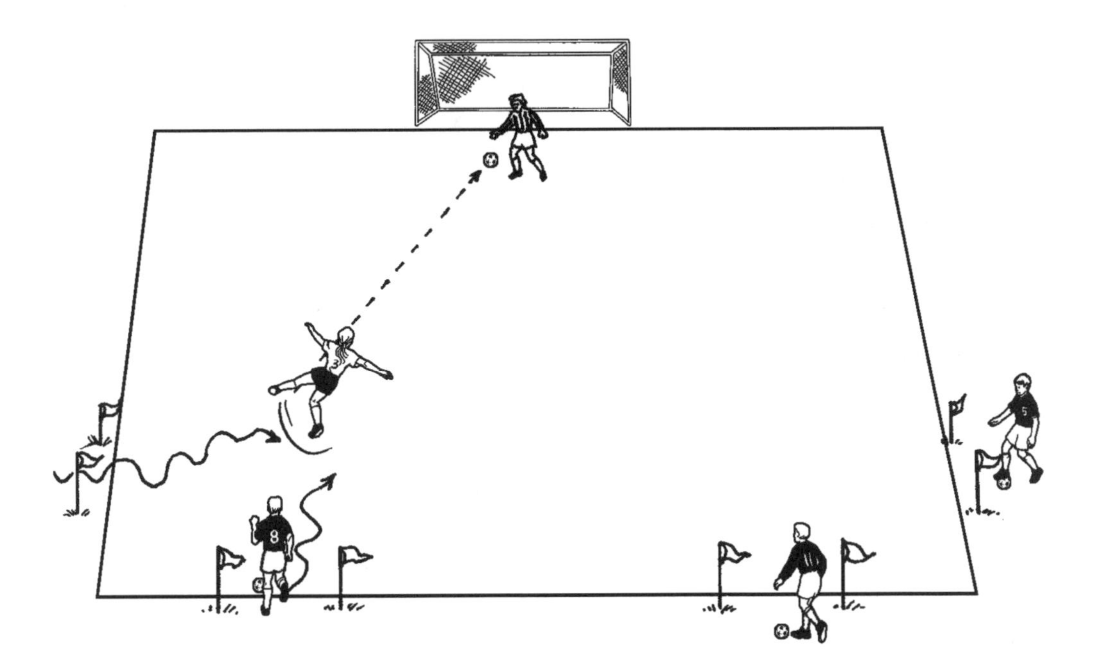

**Minutes:** 15-20

**Players:** 5 (4 shooters; 1 goalkeeper)

**Objectives:** To improve angle play; to provide shot-saving practice

**Setup:** Play on one end of a regulation field. Use flags to represent four three-yard-wide gates, one at each corner of the front edge of the penalty area and one on each side of the penalty arc. Station a shooter with a ball behind each gate. The goalkeeper positions in the goal.

**Procedure:** Shooters, in turn, dribble through their respective gate and shoot on goal. The goalkeeper advances off the line to narrow the shooting angle and make the save. After each shot or save, the goalkeeper returns to his or her original position, sets in the ready position, and prepares to save the next shot. Complete the shooting circuit twice (eight shots total), regroup, and repeat.

**Scoring:** Goalkeeper scores 1 point for each save. Shooters get 2 points for a goal scored. The player scoring the most points wins the round. Play at least five rounds.

**Practice tips:** Focus on proper footwork and optimal positioning to reduce the shooting angle. The keeper should set his or her feet just prior to the shot.

# 117 Target Practice

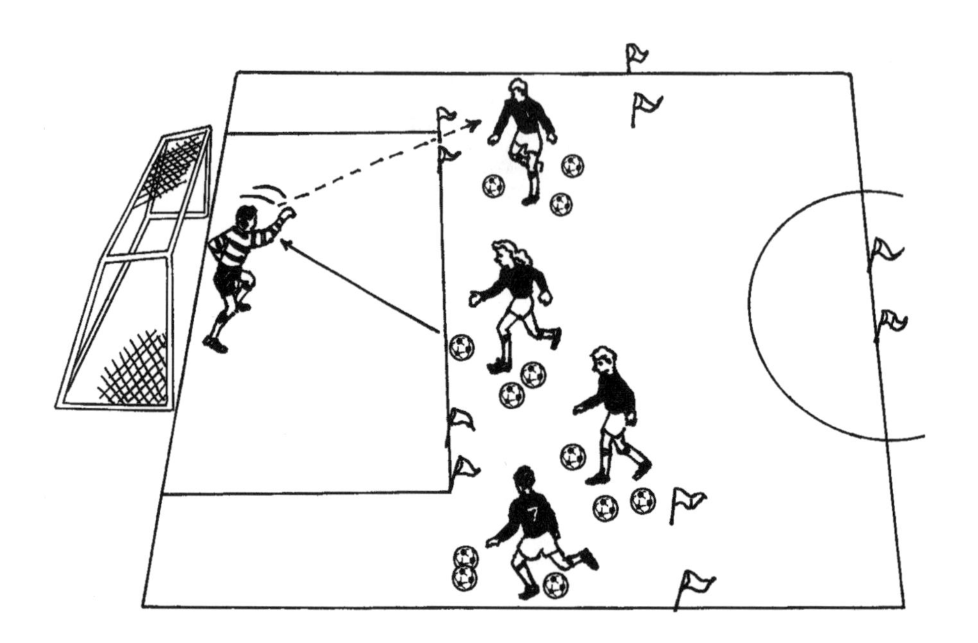

**Minutes:** 15

**Players:** 6 (4 servers; 2 goalkeepers)

**Objective:** To improve throwing accuracy

**Setup:** Play on one-half of a regulation field. Position flags to represent five 3-yard-wide goals. Position one goal within the center circle, one on each flank area about 35 yards from the endline, and one at each front corner of the penalty area. One goalkeeper stations in the goal, and the other rests to the side. Station servers at various spots outside of the penalty area, each with a supply of balls.

**Procedure:** Servers, in turn, take shots at the goal. After each save, the keeper distributes the ball by throwing it through one of the mini-goals. Continue the exercise until the keeper has attempted three tosses at each mini-goal for a total of 15 throws. After a brief pause, repeat the round with a different goalkeeper in goal. Play five rounds for each keeper.

**Scoring:** Award 1 point for a ball tossed through either of the goals positioned at the edge of the penalty area, 2 points for a ball tossed through the flank goals, and 3 points for a ball tossed directly through the goal in the center circle. The goalkeeper scoring the most points wins.

**Practice tips:** Goalkeepers can choose from several throwing techniques. The rolling (bowling) or sidearm technique can be used over short distances, whereas the baseball- or javelin-throw should be used to distribute the ball over medium and long distances. This game is not appropriate for young players who do not possess the physical strength and ability to throw the ball over distance.

# 118 Distribution Circuit

**Minutes:** 20

**Players:** 4

**Objective:** To distribute the ball accurately over various distances

**Setup:** Play on a regulation field with a full-size goal on the endline. Goalkeeper A stations in the goal, B positions outside of the penalty area near a touchline, C stations within the center circle, and D positions in the opposite penalty area. Goalkeeper A has an ample supply of balls.

**Procedure:** Begin with goalkeeper A distributing a ball to keeper B, either by the rolling or sidearm-throw technique. Keeper B receives the ball and sends it to keeper C using the baseball-throw technique. Keeper C receives the ball and distributes to keeper D via the javelin throw. Keeper D returns the ball to keeper A by dropkicking or punting it the length of the field. Keepers repeat the circuit five times, then rotate positions and repeat. Play until each keeper has taken a turn at each station.

**Scoring:** Award 1 point for an accurate throw and 2 points for an accurate punt or dropkick. By definition, accurate distribution means that the target does not have to move more than three steps in any direction to receive the ball. The goalkeeper scoring the most points wins.

**Practice tips:** Focus on proper execution of distribution techniques. Accuracy is more important than distance in most situations. This exercise is appropriate for physically mature, experienced goalkeepers of high school age and older.

# 119 Two Keepers (2-Sided Goal)

**Minutes:** 20

**Players:** 8 (2 teams of 3; 2 goalkeepers)

**Objectives:** To develop shot-saving ability; to improve angle play; to develop mobility and footwork

**Setup:** Use markers to create a 40-yard square field. Position four flags to form a 2-yard by 8-yard rectangle in the center of the field. Each 8-yard length of the rectangle represents a regulation-width goal. Form two teams of three field players. Use colored vests to differentiate teams. Station a goalkeeper on each side of the two-sided goal. One keeper has the ball.

**Procedure:** The goalkeeper with the ball tosses it to a far corner of the area, where teams vie for possession. Regular soccer rules apply, except that scores can occur through either side of the goal. Goalkeepers are neutral and attempt to save all shots. After each save, or goal scored, play is restarted, the goalkeeper tossing the ball to a corner of the area.

**Scoring:** A shot traveling between the goalposts below the height of the goalkeeper's head counts as a goal scored. The team scoring the most goals wins.

**Practice tips:** Keepers will need to make all types of saves in this game (breakaways, reaction saves, diving saves, etc.). For younger goalkeepers, designate neutral zones on each side goal where attacking players may not enter. This helps prevent collisions between field players and the goalkeeper.

# 120 High-Ball Training

**Minutes:** 20 minutes

**Players:** 9 (team of 3; 4 servers; 2 goalkeepers)

**Objectives:** To develop goalkeeper ability to receive and control high balls served into the goal area; to develop confidence in controlling the goal area

**Setup:** Play within the penalty area with a goal centered on the endline. Position a second goal at the front edge of the penalty area, opposite the goal on the endline. Station a three-player team in the area between the two goals. Use colored vests to differentiate teams. Position two servers on each flank, outside the penalty area, each with a supply of balls. A goalkeeper positions to defend each goal.

**Procedure:** Servers take turns crossing balls into the goal areas, alternating service to one keeper and then the other. Servers are allowed to move laterally along the sideline as they serve. The three-player team attempts to score all crossed balls. There are no defenders other than the goalkeeper. Keepers receive the high ball served into their goal area and immediately distribute it to a server stationed on the opposite flank. Any ball that the keeper does not hold is a live ball, to be finished by the three-player team.

**Scoring:** The keeper conceding the fewest goals wins the game.

**Practice tips:** This exercise requires keepers to extend their range and coverage of the goal area. Keepers should be aggressive but not reckless in their efforts to get to the ball. Keepers must decide which crosses they can get to and which are out of their range.

# 121 Air Wars

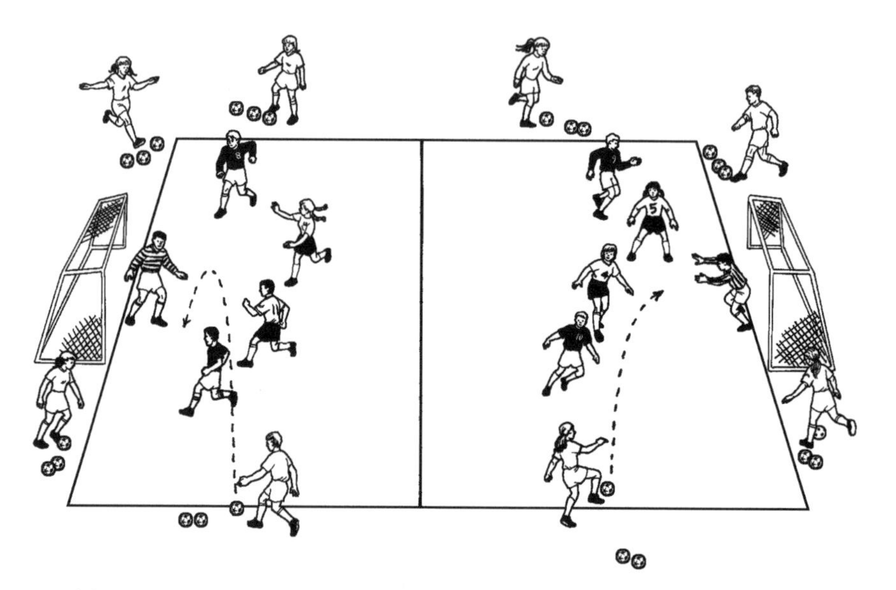

**Minutes:** 20

**Players:** 18 (2 teams of 4; 8 servers; 2 goalkeepers)

**Objective:** To provide goalkeeper training in handling a variety of high balls

**Setup:** Organize two teams of four. Use colored vests to differentiate teams. Use markers to form a playing area of 40 yards by 50 yards, divided by a midline. Position a full-size goal on each endline. Each team defends a goal. Teams station two players in their defensive half of the field and two in the opponent's half. Two servers station outside each sideline, one on each half. Two servers also position behind each endline, one to each side of the goal. Each server has several balls at his or her disposal. A goalkeeper stations in each goal.

**Procedure:** Number the servers 1 through 8 and establish a sequence (order) in which they will serve balls. Play begins with a server lofting a high ball into the goal area. Sideline servers drive their serves into the nearest goal area. Endline servers lob their serves into the far goal area. Teams play 2 v 2 in each half. Defending players try to clear the ball out of their goal area, while attacking players attempt to head or volley the ball past the keeper. The goalkeeper should attempt to play all high balls, either by catching the ball or palming it over the bar out of danger. Once a ball is cleared away, headed or volleyed into the goal, or secured by the goalkeeper, the next serve is taken. Continue for a total of 20 serves into each goal, rest, and repeat.

**Scoring:** The keeper conceding the fewest goals wins.

**Practice tips:** Keepers must control as much of the goal area as they can, yet they should not take reckless chances that might cost their team a goal. Each goal-keeper must determine his or her limits and play within them.

# 122 Breakaway Line

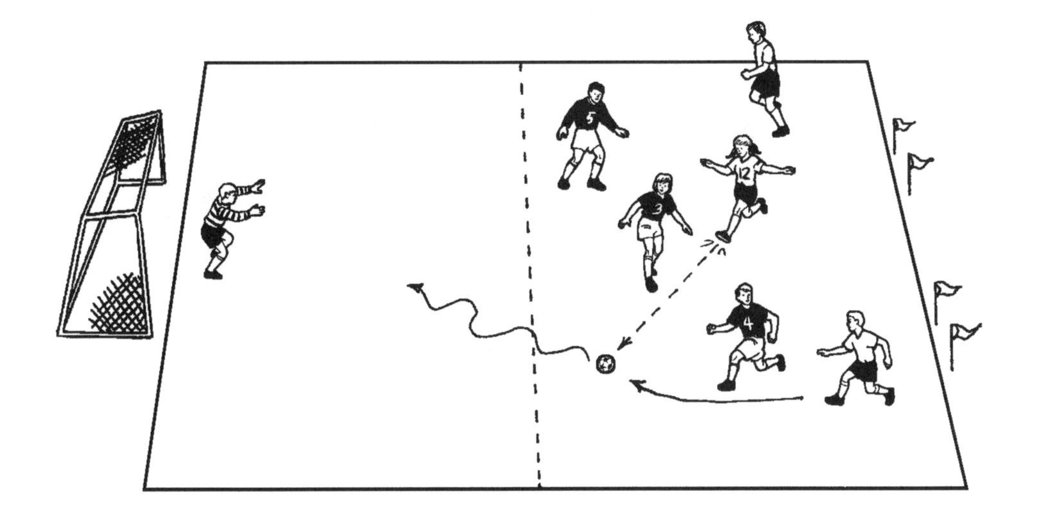


**Minutes:** 20

**Players:** 7 (2 teams of 3; 1 goalkeeper)

**Objective:** To provide goalkeeper training for breakaway situations

**Setup:** Use markers to form a 25-yard by 40-yard field area, bisected by a midline. Position a full-size goal on one endline; use flags to represent two small goals on the opposite endline. Form two teams (A and B) of three field players. One goalkeeper is required per game. Use colored vests to differentiate teams. You'll need one ball, and a supply of extra balls is recommended.

**Procedure:** Station the goalkeeper in the full-size goal. Teams A and B play 3 v 3 in the half of the field opposite the goalkeeper. Team A can score by kicking the ball through either of the two small goals on the endline; team B scores by dribbling the ball over the midline, which also serves as the breakaway line. When a player from team B dribbles across the breakaway line, he or she continues to advance at the goalkeeper in a breakaway situation, without interference. After the attempt on goal, regardless of whether the shot results in a goal scored or a save, the player immediately returns to the opposite half of the field, where play resumes. Play two 15-minute halves. Teams reverse roles in second half, with team A attacking the breakaway line and team B the small goals.

**Scoring:** Award 1 point for a goal scored in the mini-goals, 1 point for a ball dribbled over the breakaway line, and 2 points for a breakaway goal scored against the goalkeeper. The team scoring the most points wins.

**Practice tips:** As a variation, allow one defending player to chase after the attacker on the breakaway.

# 123 Two Keepers (Four Goals)

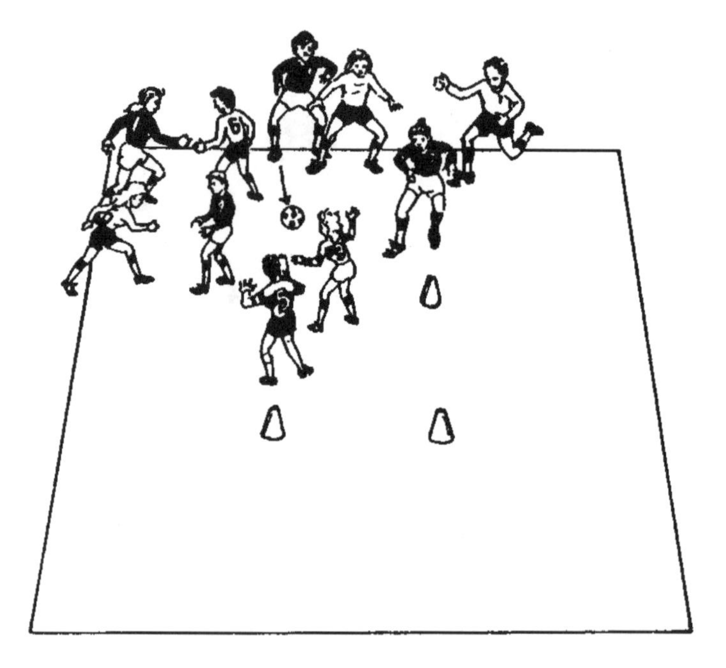

**Minutes:** 20

**Players:** 10 (2 teams of 4; 2 goalkeepers)

**Objectives:** To develop shot-saving ability; to improve mobility and footwork; to improve angle play

**Setup:** Organize two teams of four field players and two goalkeepers. Use colored vests to differentiate teams. Use markers to create a 40-yard square field area. Position four cones in the center of the area to represent the corners of an 8-yard square. Each side of the square represents a goal. You'll need one ball per game; an extra supply of balls is recommended. Give one team the ball to begin.

**Procedure:** Begin with a throw-in from outside the area. Each team must defend two adjacent sides of the square. Goals can be scored through the other two sides. Shots can be taken from any distance and any angle. The goalkeeper must defend the team's two adjacent goals and must shift from one to the other depending on the movement of the ball. Regular soccer rules apply except that the offside law is waived.

**Scoring:** The goalkeeper allowing the fewest goals wins.

**Practice tips:** Goalkeepers use the side-shuffle foot movement when moving laterally to position for a save and when moving from one goal to another. Keepers do not cross their legs when moving laterally.

# 124 High Balls Only

**Minutes:** 25

**Players:** 14 (2 teams of 6; 2 goalkeepers)

**Objectives:** To receive and control high balls; to coordinate group attack and defense

**Setup:** Organize two teams, each with a goalkeeper. Use markers to form a rectangular field area 70 yards by 50 yards. Position cones or flags to mark an 8-yard square "goal box" near each endline of the area. Station a goalkeeper in each goal box. Use colored vests to differentiate teams. You'll need one ball per game; an extra supply of balls is recommended. Give one team the ball to begin.

**Procedure:** Begin with a kickoff from the center of the field. Teams defend the goal box on their end of the field and score points by serving (kicking) the ball into the opponent's goal box so that the goalkeeper can receive the ball directly out of the air. Keepers can't leave the goal box to receive the ball in their hands, although they can move outside the box to use their feet to control a rolling ball. A ball received directly out of the air is distributed immediately to a teammate, and play continues. Other than the method of scoring, regular soccer rules are in effect. Goalkeepers may receive back passes from their teammates, although they must play these balls with their feet (in accordance with FIFA rules).

**Scoring:** Teams get 1 point for each ball received directly out of the air by the opposing goalkeeper. The team scoring the most points wins.

**Practice tips:** The goalkeeper should receive the ball at the highest possible point. Allow field players to serve (shoot) the ball from anywhere on the field. Encourage defending players to use tight marking of opponents to prevent long-range scores.

# 125 Dominate the Goal Box

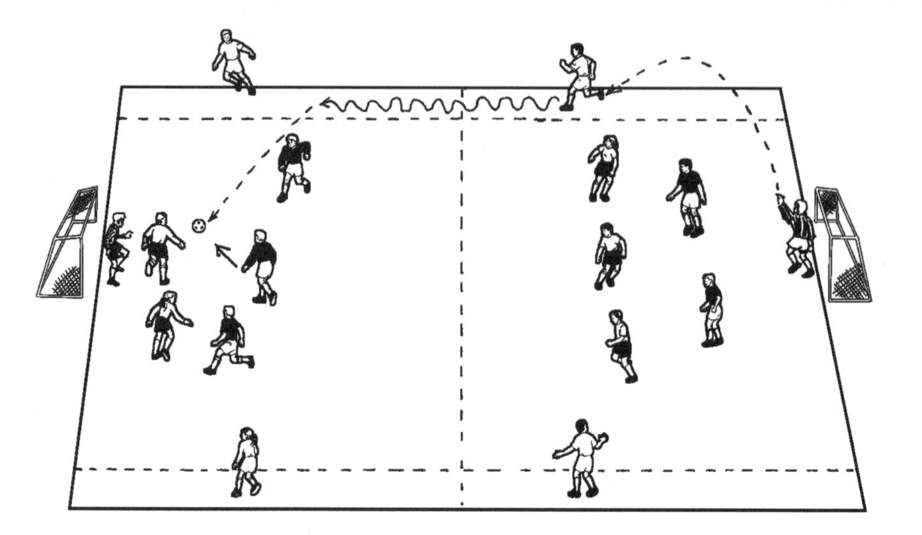

**Minutes:** 20

**Players:** 16 (4 flank players; 6 attackers, 4 defenders; 2 goalkeepers)

**Objectives:** To develop goalkeeper ability to receive and control balls crossed into the goal area; to coordinate play of the goalkeeper and defending teammates; to distribute the ball accurately by throwing

**Setup:** Use markers to form a 65-yard by 80-yard field area divided by a halfway line. Position a regulation goal on each endline. Place markers a few yards in from each sideline to create a channel for unopposed flank players. Station two flank players in each channel. Station three attackers and two defenders in each half. Station a goalkeeper in each goal, with a supply of balls. Goalkeeper A has the ball to begin. Use colored vests to differentiate teams.

**Procedure:** Keeper A tosses the ball to a flank player in either channel, who immediately dribbles down the channel toward the opposite goal and serves the ball into the goal area. The three attackers in that half of the field attempt to finish the cross, while the two defenders try to clear the ball out of the goal area. Once goalkeeper B secures the ball, he or she distributes it to a flank player on the opposite side channel of the field, who dribbles at speed toward the opposite endline and serves the ball into the goal area. A crossed ball not secured by the goalkeeper is considered a live ball and can be finished by the attacking team. Play continues for 20 minutes.

**Scoring:** The goalkeeper who concedes the fewest goals wins the game.

**Practice tips:** Keepers should distribute the ball to flank players stationed on the opposite side of the field from where the cross originated. To make the game more challenging for the goalkeeper, allow flank players to dribble inward from their wide channel to create a live 4 v 2 situation to goal. This requires additional adjustments for the goalkeeper.

# About the Author

**Joe Luxbacher** has more than 30 years of experience playing and coaching soccer at all levels. A former professional soccer player for the North American Soccer League, American Soccer League, and Major Indoor Soccer League, Luxbacher has been the head coach of men's soccer at the University of Pittsburgh since 1984.

Luxbacher was named Big East Athletic Conference Coach of the Year in 1992 and 1995, and he was selected for the Beadling Soccer Club Hall of Fame in 1995. Luxbacher earned his PhD from the University of Pittsburgh in 1985 with specializations in physical education and management as well as administration of athletics. Joe is the author of *Attacking Soccer*, *Soccer: Steps to Success*, and *The Soccer Goalkeeper, Third Edition*. He lives in Pittsburgh, Pennsylvania.